Y0-DCI-520

THE 64 TRANSPORT SERIES

The FIGHTING ROVERS

L. Geary

IAN HENRY
1983

Copyright c 1983, L. Geary

ISBN 0 86025 870 X

Made and printed in Great Britain by
Robert Hartnoll Ltd. Bodmin, Cornwall
for Ian Henry Publications Ltd
38 Parkstone Avenue, Hornchurch, Essex RM11 3LW

CONTENTS

Introduction

During the two world wars, there was always a place for the small, highly-manoeuvrable vehicle that would transport equipment and supplies, perform ambulance duties, even carry a limited number of fully-equipped troops or personnel over all kinds of terrain, and also act in scout and commander car roles both in the field and at Headquarters.

The versatile Ford model 'T' fitted this role to a degree during the Great War. Whilst it did achieve magnificent results, it could get into a situation where an all-wheel drive, had such a version been available, would have encountered no difficulties, but at that time automobile engineering was in its infancy.

Little had been accomplished during the peace-time years that followed the 1914-18 conflict in providing a versatile small vehicle for military purposes.

When the Second World War came it was realised that automobile transportation for the Services, both fighting and domestic, was of vital importance.

It was during this conflict that such a vehicle found its place, accomplishing its duties and giving a near-perfect solution: the American Willys' Jeep (Jeep standing for G.P. – general purpose), an all-wheel drive lightweight wonder.

Until the Jeep was issued to the British forces, their lightweight vehicles, ranging from 5cwt to 15cwt capacity, were based upon the lighter end of the commercial vehicle manufacturers' models of civilian machines, which was the obvious way of giving a quick wartime transport system.

It was after the war, in 1948, that a remarkable machine was launched at the Amsterdam Motor Show on 30th April as the 'Farmers' Friend', to be followed with appearances during the same year in other shows in Ulster and Bath. The name of the vehicle – the "Land-Rover".

The Rover Company, as most of the British motor industry in 1946, began after World War II to find itself in difficulties due to the change-over from war- to peace-time civilian production.

Because of the shortage of sheet steel that provided material for motor car bodies and other commodities using panellings, the Government allocated available stocks and production to companies within industries that were able to secure large export orders.

The Rover Company, whilst having a fine reputation for producing high quality motor cars, unfortunately only had a reasonable export market, only a small proportion of its cars being sold overseas.

The foundation of the fantastic four-wheel drive Land Rover was the result of a meeting between the Managing Director of the Rover Company, Spencer Wilks, and another director, Maurice Wilks, to discuss the policy for the future of their car production and what could be done to improve their export potential. They both agreed that something had to be done to maintain their new factories at Tyseley and Solihull with work, otherwise there were going to be some unemployed hands. Solihull was a shadow factory built in 1939 to ensure that the company had a base in the event of their Coventry plant being destroyed during the war [which did happen in November, 1940]. There was one other idea in Maurice Wilks' mind: he required a work horse for his farm, a vehicle between a tractor and a light truck or pick-up. He had acquired an ex-War Office vehicle, an American Willys' Jeep. Now this vehicle had been doing great work on the farm and giving good service, but it was getting worn out. Maurice Wilks was left with two options: first, to purchase another ex-WD Jeep; secondly, design and build such a vehicle in the Rover plant.

American Jeep, 1939-45

The disadvantage of the first option was that the second Jeep would become worn out eventually and spares would not be very easy to obtain. The second choice would, if successful, provide work for their factories. The brothers agreed after considering the pros and cons, and convinced themselves that there must be a market for this type of vehicle. Surely other farmers and even contractors must be in the same predicament, wanting a replacement vehicle or tractor. They started on the project of producing a prototype similar to the American Jeep. From a finance point of view, there would be no funds availale for such a project or any other concept in motor car design. Production would be on existing vehicles made pre-war, until money and materials were available.

Components from the Rover motor cars already in production would have to be used to their fullest extent. There was a suitable engine, the new 1.6 litre unit being developed for the P3 Rover 60. The gearbox, rear axle and other parts were considered, but a new transfer gearbox and a front drive axle would be required, also probably a new chassis frame. For the body, this could be styled using flat panels with square or simple bend corners; no special tooling would be needed.

Light alloys, such as aluminium, could be used wherever possible. To commence the first prototype another Jeep was purchased and stripped down. The chassis frame, suitably modified, was used, also the transfer gearbox and the front wheel drive axle. Central steering wheel position was introduced as for a tractor. However, after testing the prototype, this steering wheel position was found to be unsatisfactory and it was relocated to the right hand side with provision for a left hand drive when required.

The vehicle became an immediate winner with the help of the Government's decision to classify the machine as an agricultural vehicle, thereby becoming free of Purchase Tax that was imposed on motor cars and other goods at that time.

In 1950 a new gearbox was introduced which eliminated the free wheel device and provided optional two or four wheel drive in high ratio, with four wheel drive permanently in low gear of the transfer gearbox.

Development of the Land Rover vehicle continues for both military and civilian requirements.

Military Adoption

For the British forces, light commercial vehicles ranging from 5cwt to 15cwt capacities were based on the commercial vehicle manufacturers' pre-war models, suitably modified.

Morris Commercial, Vauxhall (Bedford), and Ford had produced large quantities of the 15cwt capacity general purpose vehicle and infantry trucks during World War II. These vehicles, whilst being extremely useful, were still too large and heavy for the manoeuvrability needed and were limited in the terrain wherein they could operate. All-wheel drive versions of 3 tons and 30 cwt capacities were engineered, but, again, the basis was a standard commercial vehicle very good for rapid supply of transport to the fighting forces. All these vehicles did a magnificent job during the hostilities, but were too heavy to be used as advanced units and scout cars in modern warfare.

To design and develop a machine suitable would require time which was not readily available at the height of the conflict. Fortunately, the U.S.Army had the answer in the Willys' Jeep, a lightweight all-wheel drive vehicle, easily manoeuvrable, easily transported, and quick in action: the almost-perfect scout car.

Land Rovers of a Reconnaisance Platoon of the Royal Highland Fusiliers.

The military side of the Land Rover really commenced when, during the Second World War, the American Jeep was being shipped in large numbers to the British and Allied forces. The War Department and the Ministry of Supply started investigating the motor industry for a British designed and built machine, the equivalent of the Jeep, to save dollars that could be put to other use.

This proposition was submitted to the motor industry for them to study and submit designs and possible prototypes to the Fighting Vehicle Research and Development Establishment (F.V.R.D.E.) for inspection, testing and, finally, acceptance for military service. The idea was to design and produce such a vehicle as could accommodate the maximum number of commercial major components, such as engine, gearbox, rear axle, etc.

The project was known as FV1800, a specially developed vehicle to be used as a combat machine that could be placed with the fighting forces at short notice: in other words, the Army required a British Jeep.

Morris, Austin and the Rootes Group became involved, with the Nuffield Group undertaking the design work and the other companies providing the major components. By the end of hostilities in Europe a prototype stage had been achieved.

After the formation of the British Motor Corporation, between Morris and Austin, the FV1800 was put into production in 1952 by the Austin group, but the development had taken a great deal longer than was at first anticipated.

The FV1800 did not result in a straightforward design, but it certainly was a special vehicle developed for combat forces.

I believe that the Rover Company did not participate in this venture, as only small numbers were anticipated for the military requirements now that the war was over. Also there would be very little appeal for civilian use, having the lack of payload space. Maurice Wilks could have had a great deal of interest in this initial project — had the quantities been large enough to keep his factories in work.

During this time, the Land Rover was rapidly gaining good markets and a very good reputation. The F.V.R.D.E. had already taken three machines from the first batch of production of the Land Rover as early as 1948.

After a long inspection and investigation, the Establishment had come to the conclusion that this machine was not to be ignored and had great possibilities. It had potential, even though it was not specially designed, built, or even considered for military use. But it was small and reliable, also very manoeuvrable.

F.V.D.R.E. prepared a Land Rover and compared it with the FV1800. The latter was more adaptable in this line of operation and was more agile than the Land Rover. On the other hand, the Land Rover was a regular commercial production machine, it was cheaper and had commercially produced components readily available for maintenance. This must have been a great advantage and, with modifications to suit military specifications, gave the British forces the machine they wanted In the event of hostilities, the Land Rover could be produced in numbers without any special and expensive tooling.

In 1949 an order for a small number of vehicles was placed by the Ministry to the Rover Company for Land Rovers modified to suit the F.V.R.D.E. specifications. These were probably distributed within the Army for a trail period. The trials were evidently successful, as a substantial order for several hundred followed later. The vehicle had to be satisfied with its duties behind the front line as an all purpose vehicle for Headquarters and other services, such as the Royal Navy and the Royal Air Force as transport.

Between 1950 and 1952 Land Rovers went into action in Korea. Here they proved themselves, being more versatile than the FV1800s, in spite of having less power. Their advantage, however, was their ability to carry stores, equipment, and personnel or any combination of the three. When the first Land Rovers were given a trial with the forces, experience gained suggested that really the army wanted more capacity and power. This they received in 1952 and 1954 with engine and wheelbase changes. It was in the mid-1950s that the FV1800 ceased production, thus leaving the Land Rover to hold its own with virtually a clear field.

A further increase in the standard wheel base was implemented in 1956 to 2.23 metres (88 inches), followed by the long wheelbase increased to 2.77 metres (109 inches). This would give the forces extra space for the payload.

There was still the problem of towing a small gun or trailer. With the increase in payload as well as creating heavy rear axle and loading, this proved too great for the standard rear axle assembly. A stronger rear axle was needed, so a Salisbury type was introduced to obviate the strains caused by towing.

To satisfy the W.D. Vehicle Specifications, inaugurated by the F.V.R.D.E., additions and modifications were carried out on the standard Land Rover. These were –

F.V. design of towing hook and reinforced rear cross member.
W.O. pattern divided road wheels.
Tyres – various sizes – cross country tread pattern and sand tyres.
Twin fuel tanks.
Vehicle lashing eyes.
Freight lashing cleats.
Rear bumper.
Modified front bumpers for pushing trailers, etc.
Oil cooler
Eight bladed fan.
F.V. pattern lights.
Electrical system – 12 or 24 volts, whichever was needed.
Mounting points to be provided to accept wireless installation in an emergency.

Linemen of the Royal Corps of Signals lay telephone cable from a Land Rover

For the Fitted for Radio vehicles the following extras must be included
-
  24 volt 40 amp/hour rectifier A.C. electrical system with provision for charging wireless batteries
  Full suppression equipment to F.V.R.D.E. Specification 2051
  Built in equipment for radio role, including the following -
    wireless table
    battery carrier
    two batteries
    co-axial aerial leads
    operator's seat, etc.

7

Other items necessary for carrying out special duties would include –
  ambulance equipment
  aircraft crash rescue equipment
  airportable flotation kits
  water purifying equipment, etc.
To provide more power a new 2.286 litre (139.4 cu.ins) overhead valve petrol engine was introduced and, three years later, a diesel engine of the same capacity.
A general service truck of ½ ton capacity with the new diesel engine entered military service, appearing in the 1966 British Military Vehicle Exhibition at Chertsey. A previous unit was used as a prototype with this diesel engine by F.V.R.D.E. for vehicle (Land Rover) maintenance in the field.
After the war, production of the 5cwt light utility truck, such as the Austin 10 h.p. Utility; the Hillman 'Minx' Utility; and the Morris 'M' Utility, ceased. These vehicles had now been replaced by the Land Rover. The 15cwt general service and infantry truck, such as Ford, Morris, Austin, Vauxhall (Bedford) and Commer ceased production. None of these vehicles was considered by the vehicle manufacturers to create a civilian market, so that they could be retained for the Services. The other W.D. vehicles that continued for a short time were the four wheel drive machines; the Humber 4 x 4 8cwt personnel/general service and the Morris PU 8/4 8cwt 4 x 4 truck, but these were larger and heavier than was required, also there was no intention to continue with the civilian types in production, so these also ceased. This now left the Services looking for further operational duties for the Land Rover: after successes at ¼ ton plus rating, could a 15cwt version be achieved?
The ¾ ton version was planned and also proved successful in service as a cargo vehicle and a general service F.F.R. machine. Powered by the same 2.286 litre petrol engine as the ¼ ton. 7.50 x 16 tyres of the light truck type with cross country tread pattern on 5.50E x 16 rims were fitted, with 9.00 x 15 ribbed desert pattern tread tyres on 6.0L x 15 W/BR pattern rims offered as optional equipment. A total load complement of 1,030 kgs (2,080 lb) giving a gross vehicle weight of 2,591 kgs (5,712 lb). Deeper spring brackets were fitted to the chassis frame to accommodate the large optional tyres.
The ambulance version offered accommodation for a medical attendant and two stretcher cases or, alternatively, one stretcher case and three sitting cases or, as a second alternative, six sitting patients, all in addition to the driver. Later, a heavier version, based on the ¾ ton chassis, was released for service. This version provided space for a medical attendant and up to four stretcher cases or, alternatively, up to two stretcher cases and three sitting patients and with the same second alternative as the lighter versions, of six sitting patients, again all in addition to the driver.
To assist in the protection of aircraft an Aircraft Crash Rescue Unit was released in line to meet the Air Ministry's requirements for a

vehicle for immediate rescue from crashed aircraft; to deal with aircraft wheel brake fires, and to act as a light auxiliary truck to escort
aircraft to dispersals.

To achieve vehicle air transportation, a 1 ton airportable general service
machine was required; this was accomplished by upgrading the $\frac{3}{4}$ ton
machine and fitting a special body to the standard 2.77 metre (109.0
inch) wheelbase Land Rover chassis. The laden weight was 2,970 kgs
(6,548 lb) within the capabilities of the vehicle. Three of these machines could be stacked, one on top of the other, to provide a minimum
bulk of load within the aircraft.The vehicle was capable of transporting
eight fully equipped troops or one ton of stores in both cases in
addition to the driver.

Various roles were carried out by the $\frac{1}{4}$ ton general service truck
version, such a role was the accommodation of the equipment for Line
Laying

Royal Marines pictured during jungle training exercises

9

For a more advanced type of weapon the anti-tank missile, the Vigilant, the equipment could be fitted on to an open type Land Rover of ¾ ton capacity, consisting of a specially designed carrier frame that could launch two missiles from the vehicle.

An unusual role for the Land Rover was that of an amoured patrol car. This version was based on the standard Land Rover 2.77 metre (109 inch) wheelbase, with a welded armoured plate body fitted. The vehicle carried a crew of three and was designed to fulfil economically a wide variety of duties, such as border patrols, convoy escort, reconnaissance and internal security roles. It was also fitted with a 0.30 inch Browning machine gun with turret mounted smoke projector if required. The British Military General Staff considered that it would be a great advantage if a vehicle such as the Land Rover could be dropped by parachute near front line operation. This scheme certainly sounded good, but unfortunately it was not feasible. It had been tried with a Jeep with very unsatisfactory results; a rather bent and battered vehicle lying on the ground. Nothing was really accomplished in this field until a fleet of large helicopters came into the picture on supportive military activities. To successfully be airportable, the Land Rover needed to be as light as possible; somewhere near to 1,134 kgs (2,500 lb) unladen weight. It is possible that this weight was the safe load that the helicopters could lift.

The vehicle was initially to be based on the general service truck version of the ¼ ton with the 2.23 metre (88.0 inch) wheelbase. Whilst the long wheelbase at 2.77 metres (109.0 inch) gave better stores or equipment space, it was impossible to try to reduce this model to anywhere near the required weight.

Austin had already been approached to submit a design and prototype. Their vehicle embodied the engine, transmission and suspension units

from their 1100 range of motor cars. The vehicle body gave accommodation for a driver and three passengers or, alternatively, a driver and 362 kgs (800 lb) of cargo. Independent suspension was fitted on all four wheels by means of torsion bars. The engine assembly was transversly mounted at the front of the vehicle with the radiator at the left hand side, with a cooler pusher fan expelling air into the wheelarch. Normal drive was at the front wheels only. Four wheel drive and low range were engaged independently. Its unladen weight was 727 kgs (1,598 lb) and the gross weight 1,181 kgs (2,598 lb). Very good, but, as shown in the photograph, the vehicle was too low, very little belly clearance, so necessary in military operations.

To bring the Land Rover down to weight meant stripping the short wheelbase $\frac{1}{4}$ ton vehicle completely. Then it had to be rebuilt with only items necessary to make the machine mobile. Such items as the doors, the windscreen, the body construction with sides, tailboard, front and rear mudguards, and seats were not needed. The vehicle finally finished as a chassis equipped with a restyled front end sheet metal work, a floor pan and seat risers. The styling changed to simplify the shape and reduce the weight of the front end grille. Flat sheet top cover plates were fixed to the sides of the bonnet to cover the tyres and accommodate the front side lights and flasher units, the headlights were

A specially adapted $\frac{3}{4}$ ton Land Rover in use as a Commander's Vehicle, pictured at the Royal Army Ordnance Corps Vehicle Depot in Belgium

fitted in the grille. An open end load platform was made and three seating capacity was given by a lightweight bench seat. The unladen weight was reduced to 1,406 kgs (3,100 lb), complete with 90.86 litres (20 gallons) of fuel. The bare weight would be approximately 1,335 kgs (2,940 lb). The cargo weight capable of being carried was 589 kgs (1,298 lb) against the Austin's 362 kgs (800 lb) and had more power. Further reductions could be possible. It was now necessary to engineer the project for production. A new styled front end similar to the prototype with flat panels and small radiused corners. A very stark body was provided, consisting of a simple swept up and down frame, floor pan and seat risers. It was so designed that the doors, windscreen assembly, upper body, tailgate panels could be added to form a serviceable vehicle weighing 2,018 kgs (4,480 lb). The stark basic vehicle, with further parts discarded, could be helicopter lifted or air transported and the extras dropped as separate package(s) to be assembled on landing.

The vehicle was available with 12 volt or 24 volt electrical systems, the latter to be had with up to 90 amp/hour alternators. All 24 volt vehicles were fully suppressed, meeting the military operational standards. The vehicle was fitted with a full length soft top constructed of rot-proof, flame retardant canvas, supported by a galvanised set of struts. Twin fuel tanks were fitted underneath the seats, and provided with one telescopic filler neck to facilitate filling from jerrycans. It was classified by the Ministry and the F.V.R.D.E. as a ½ ton machine.

On the general service truck version could be mounted a 106 mm (4.173 inch) anti-tank gun. This gun-carrying version had been specially designed using the ½ ton G.S. truck chassis as a basis, to meet the demand for the fitting of the gun. The vehicle retained all the high mobility characteristics of the conventional Land Rover, with the added advantage of airportability. The result was a tactically versatile unit capable of operating in all types of terrain – sandy, swampy, mountainous – with a range of action of 600 kilometres (372.6 miles) and a maximum road speed of 90 kilometres per hour (56 mph). The machine can assume a strategic position quickly and unobtrusively, fire in any forward direction (180 degree arc of fire) and swiftly move to assume another position.

The latest version (1981/2), still classified as a ½ ton 4 x 4 general service vehicle, had an unladen weight of 1,450 kgs (3,197 lb), inclusive of 90.86 litres (20 gallons) of fuel and some other additional items; payload of 406 kgs (895 lb), plus driver and one passenger. However, for airportability and helicopter lifting, the unladen weight was capable of being further reduced to a stark vehicle of 1,225 kgs (2,701 lb).

The ¾ ton Land Rover proved particularly suitable to be adapted to many duties. The ambulance version has already been noticed and new versions have been introduced, such as an armoured patrol car and an armoured personnel carrier in 1980 constructed on a ¾ ton heavy duty chassis by Short Brothers, Ltd., of Belfast. The personnel carrier had

Armoured patrol cars on scouting exercises. Land Rover 2.77 metres wheelbase with special armour plate. Body by Short Brothers, Belfast.

added protection against rifle and machine gun fire, whilst transporting up to eight personnel.

Another special conversion of the $\frac{3}{4}$ ton long wheelbase heavy duty chassis was the Laird (Anglesey) Centaur, a new range of half track machines, with a Rover engine of 3.50 litres (213.58 cu.in.) petrol and the Range Rover transmission. The half track system was that of the Scorpion CVR(T) vehicles. This vehicle carried out special duties such as mine laying, missile carrier, ambulance and command vehicle. It has a payload of 3,090 kgs (6,720 lb).

A further duty carried out by the $\frac{3}{4}$ ton version was that of a field artillery computer equipment vehicle (FACE). Equipped with a 24 volt electrical system, this machine is capable of being used as a command post for a Marconi FACE system. The artillery fire direction system consists of three elements: FACE computer equipment, ALICE (Artillery Line Communications Equipment) carried in the Land Rover and the AWDATS (Artillery Weapons Data Transmission System). The FACE consul can deal with up to 24 guns and rocket battery. There seems to be no end to the variety of work to which the Land Rover can be put.

Again, another specialist, the British Aerospace Anti-tank Missile System, wire guided anti-tank missile, the 'Swingfire'. The pallet mounted 'Beeswing' launcher was installed in the read of the vehicle and is fired using a remote controller.

A half-track Centaur Land Rover being used by the 17/21st Lancers on cold weather trials in northern Norway

Although the range had been extended with the introduction of the $\frac{3}{4}$ ton version, cargo space was not sufficient to accommodate the ever-increasing bulky and heavy equipment. Even a 2.77 metre (109.0 inch) wheelbase was inadequate. The towing capacity wanted was in the region of 1,814 kgs (4,000 lb) to cater for cargoes of various types and a medium size gun. A major decision had to be made.
The additional need for towing the new 105 mm light gun was an important requirement.
Existing Land Rovers had been tested for towing capabilities, but proved inadequate. An alternative of having power-driven trailers and gun carriage was considered. In 1966 a 2.77 metre (109.0 inch) wheelbase Land Rover and a Scottorn power driven axle trailer were available commercially and were under assessment in aid of a Ministry of Defence (Royal Air Force) requirement for a light tactical airportable fire appliance and for research. An additional transfer gearbox was put at the rear of the vehicle, coupled to the power take-off on the main gearbox to give the driving facility to the trailer, which was fitted with a driving axle basically common to the rear axle of the towing vehicle – that had to be of the same ratio. Drive from the vehicle to the trailer axle was by means of two telescopic tubular propeller shafts

¾ ton Land Rover undergoing reliability tests with Scottern trailer

with a single universal joint at each end. The shaft coupling the trailer to the towing vehicle could be quickly detached.

The total weight of the train was 4,000 kgs (8,796 lb) and an unladen weight of 2,030 kgs (4,476 lb).

However, this was not really satisfactory, even when tried with extra power by fitting the Rover six cylinder petrol engine with suitable corresponding transmission line installed. This proved to be too heavy to be considered for air-lift.

A new machine was needed, a forward control version to cater for the maximum cargo space and of 1 ton capacity payload.

The F.V.R.D.E. issued a specification with the desired wheelbase, tracks, clearances, and the appropriate departure and approach angles. Payload and power weight ratio requirements were also spelt out. The rest was left to the motor industry to submit a suitable machine. A forward control Land Rover 4 x 4 was subjected to assessment trials at the Establishment at Chertsey.

The vehicle was a commercial development based on the then current 2.77 metre (109.0 inch) wheelbase ¾ ton general service truck. The cab had been moved to a position over the front axle and raised, to achieve the necessary clearance with relation to the engine and the front wheels. The wheelbase was increased to 2.8 metres (110 inches). Heavy duty axles, manufactured by E.N.V.Ltd., had been fitted with a wider track for both front and rear and a wider spring centres, transversely. These wider spring centres compensated for the higher centre of gravity of the vehicle towards stability. Provision was made for the fitting of a

15

flat platform body.

The vehicle was tested with the Rover 2.286 litre engine installed. On completion of the tests and inspection, the project was considered unsatisfactory. It was rather heavy and had not the necessary power to haul the large tractor load expected across hard terrain. There can have been no doubt in Rover's mind that a completely new vehicle was required.

This new vehicle had the Range Rover's engine and transmission installed. This V8 petrol engine at 3.5 litre capacity was able to give 162 b.h.p. (121 Kw). There was an entirely new chassis, with heavier front and rear axle units. A new cab was styled, still using flat panels for easier replacement. The unladen weight was 1,860 kgs (4,101 lb) against the previously submitted conversion at 2,036 kgs (4,480 lb). A good saving in weight and a possible change of being airportable.

It was designed to meet the requirements for a high power to weight ratio, suitable for helicopter lift, a general service truck. The body had the usual lashing points, hinged and removeable side and tailboards. The 2.49 metre (98.0 inch) length and 1.727 metre (68.0 inch) width body allowed maximum use of the vehicle for specialist installations. The suspension was still the standard system of semi-elliptic leaf springs and double acting hydraulic telescopic shock absorbers. No common parts other than the engine and the gearbox from either the Land Rover or the Range Rover were used. The payload was classified as 1 metric tonne capacity.

Under development in 1966, with the old 1 ton forward control vehicle, was a 30cwt version based on the same idea, forward mounting of the standard cab. This 30cwt model was equipped with the Perkins 6.354 diesel engine of 5.8 litre capacity (354 cu.in.), a five speed gearbox and 11.00 x 16 tyres. It was submitted to meet a requirement for a general service truck of 30cwt load carrier. Front wheel drive was controlled by the driver and was available in all gear ratios. As a production model it could be fitted with a general service cargo body or, indeed, any specialist body. The load platform area was suitable for carrying a standard one ton container. Wheelbase was 2.85 metres (112.0 inches) and with an unladen weight of 3,390 kgs (7,460 lb). Laden it was 4,290 kgs (10.850 lb).

Most countries have some Land Rovers operating in their military transport fleets. A large percentage of Rover's production of the Land Rover have carried out duties in government services both home and overseas and will continue to do so.

Types of Military Versions & Specifications

In 1962 two organisations, Fighting Vehicles Research & Development Establishment (F.V.R.D.E.) and the Society of Motor Manufacturers and Traders (S.M.M.T.) staged an exhibition of British military vehicles at Chertsey. Several Land Rovers appeared in their various roles. Some were already in service with the forces and others were either under development or assessment. Below is a review of the collection at this particular exhibition —

Those already in service —
1. $\frac{1}{4}$ ton cargo 4 x 4 truck.
2. $\frac{1}{4}$ ton F F R (Fitted for radio) 4 x 4 truck.
3. $\frac{3}{4}$ ton cargo 4 x 4 truck.
4. $\frac{3}{4}$ ton F F R 4 x 4 truck.
5. $\frac{3}{4}$ ton Airfield Crash Rescue 4 x 4 truck.
6. Ambulance (2 stretcher) 4 x 4.
7. 1 ton Airportable General Purpose 4 x 4 truck.
8. 1 ton Airportable General Purpose 4 x 4 truck flotation kit for Vehicle 7.

Those under development —
9. $\frac{1}{4}$ ton cargo 4 x 4 truck (with multifuel engine).
10. 1 ton Airportable General Purpose 4 x 4 truck (Design mock-up).
11. Servicing $\frac{3}{4}$ ton 4 x 4 truck.

In 1966 the same two organisations staged a further exhibition. Again, several Land Rovers were shown in their various roles. Some were identical to those shown 4 years previously, but peculiar to the 1966 exhibition were —

Those in service —
12. $\frac{3}{4}$ ton General Service/G.W. 4 x 4 truck.
13. $\frac{1}{2}$ ton General Service 4 x 4 truck (diesel engined).
14. $\frac{1}{4}$ ton General Service 4 x 4 truck line layer.
15. $\frac{3}{4}$ ton Ambulance (2 to 4 stretcher) 4 x 4.

Those under development or assessment —
16. $\frac{1}{4}$ ton General Service Lightweight 4 x 4 truck (stripped vehicle).
17. $\frac{1}{4}$ ton General Service Lightweight 4 x 4 truck (complete vehicle).
18. $\frac{3}{4}$ ton cargo F F R 4 x 4 and power driven trailer.
19. $\frac{3}{4}$ ton cargo 4 x 4 truck (for powered trailers).
20. 1 ton cargo 4 x 4 truck (forward control).
21. $1\frac{1}{2}$ ton cargo 4 x 4 truck (forward control).

Further development on various assortments of projects with unusual vehicles went on until 1981, when the Military Vehicle and Engineering Establishment (M.V.E.E.) issued a book showing the British military vehicles in service or under development or assessment since the 1966 exhibition.

These were –

22. $\frac{1}{2}$ ton General Service 4 x 4 truck (lightweight).
23. $\frac{1}{2}$ ton General Service 4 x 4 F F R truck.
24. 1 tonne General Service 4 x 4 truck (forward control).
25. 1 tonne Ambulance (4 stretcher) 4 x 4 (forward control).

The other versions still in service are the $\frac{1}{4}$ ton and the $\frac{3}{4}$ ton versions both in cargo and F F R duties.

These are listed below –

1. $\frac{1}{4}$ ton cargo version.
2. $\frac{1}{4}$ ton F F R version.
3. $\frac{3}{4}$ ton cargo version.
4. $\frac{3}{4}$ ton F F R version.
5. $\frac{3}{4}$ ton Airfield Crash & Rescue version.

$\frac{3}{4}$ ton long wheelbase Land Rover, used as a General Purpose Command and Radio Vehicle in most Regiments of the British Army. It can tow a $\frac{1}{2}$ ton trailer

14. ¼ ton line layer version.
15. ¾ ton Ambulance version.
Alternative roles carried out by these versions are quoted at the end of each specification

The M.V.E.E. was formed in April, 1970, by an amalgamation of the F.V.R.D.E. at Chertsey and the Military Engineering Experimental Establishment (M.E.X.E.), Christchurch.

Field Artilllery Computer Equipment (FACE). The Artillery Fire Direction System has three elements: FACE computer equipment, ALICE [Artillery Line Communications Equipment] carried in the Land Rover, and AWDATS [Artillery Weapon Data Transmission System]. The FACE console can deal with up to 24 guns and is programmable by cassette for every type of gun and rocket battery

ENGINE SPECIFICATIONS

Engine No. 1

Type	Rover 2.286 litre. 4 cylinder in-line petrol (gasoline)
Bore	90.47 mm (3.56 inches)
Stroke	88.9 mm (3.5 inches)
Capacity	2,286 cc (139.498 cu.in)
Compression ratio	8.0:1
Maximum power	51.5 Kw (69 b.h.p.) @ 4,000 r.p.m.
Nett torque	157 Nm (116.0 lbft) @ 1,500 r.p.m.
Carburettor	Single Zenith 361V.
Engine lubrication	Wet sump. Full force feed.
Ignition	Coil. 12 volt
Fuel pump	Mechanical lift pump with priming lever and sediment bowl.

Engine No 2

Type	Rover 3.5 litre 8 cylinder 'V' formation (petrol) gasoline
Bore	88.9 mm (3.50 inches)
Stroke	71.1 mm (2.799 inches)
Capacity	3,528 cc (250.56 cu.in)
Compresssion ratio	8.5:1
Maximum power	121 Kw (162.26 b.h.p.) @ 5,000 r.p.m.
Nett torque	260 Nm (191,77 lbft) @ 2,500 r.p.m.
Carburettor	Not available
Engine lubrication	Wet sump. Full force feed
Ignition	Coil. 12 volt
Fuel pump	Mechanical lift pump with priming lever and sediment bowl

Engine No. 3

Type	Rover 2.286 litre 4 cylinder in line (Derv) diesel.
Bore	90.47 mm (3.56 inches)
Stroke	88.90 mm (3.5 inches)
Capacity	2,286cc (139.498 cu.in)
Compression ratio	23:1
Maximum power	41.9 Kw (56.2 b.h.p.) @ 4,000 r.p.m.
Nett torque	137.3 Nm (101.3 lbft) @ 1,800 r.p.m.
Injection pump	Self-governing C.A.V. DPA distributor type
Injectors	C.A.V. Pintaux
Engine lubrication	Wet sump. Full force feed.
Ignition	Compression ignition
Fuel pump	Mechanical lift pump with priming lever

Engine No. 4

Type	Rover 2.5 litre 4 cylinder in line Multi-fuel (Derv or petrol)
Bore/Stroke	Not available
Capacity	2,530 cc (154.4 cu.in.)
Maximum power	46.98 Kw (63 b.h.p.) @ 4,000 r.p.m.
Nett torque	264 Nm (195 lbft) @ 1,850 r.p.m.
Governed speed	4,000 r.p.m.
Injection pump	D.P.A.with pressurising pump
Injectors	C.A.V. Pintaux
Engine lubrication	Wet sump. Full force feed
Ignition	Compression ignition
Compression ratio	Not available
Fuel pump	Mechanical lift pump with priming lever

Engine No. 5

Type	Rover 3.0 litre 6 cylinder in line (petrol) gasoline
Bore	77.8 mm (3.063 inches)
Stroke	105 mm (4.134 inches)
Capacity	2,995 cc (182 cu.in.)
Compression ratio	8.75:1
Maximum power	82.06 Kw (110.0 b.h.p.) @ 4,500 r.p.m.
Nett torque	206.1 Nm (152.0 lbft) @ 1,500 r.p.m.
Carburettor	S.U. Type HD8
Engine lubrication	Wet sump. Full force feed
Ignition	Coil. 12 volt
Fuel pump	Dual electric pumps

The Scottorn 'Bushmaster' trailer drawn by a Land Rover over bad terrain

The 101 in. wheelbase forward control Land Rover GS, 1 tonne, at the Royal School of Artillery, Larkhill, Wiltshire

TRANSMISSION SPECIFICATIONS

Transmission No. 1

Clutch	Single dry plate. Diaphragm spring
Clutch diameter	241 mm (9.5 in)
Main gearbox	4 speed transmission synchro-mesh. 4 forward 1 reverse. Synchromesh on all forward gears
Main gearbox ratio	3.734:1 1st; 2.227:1 2nd; 1.494:1 3rd; 1:1 4th; 3.886:1 reverse
Transfer gearbox	2 speed reduction On main gearbox output. 2/4 wheel drive, control on transfer gearbox output.
Transfer gearbox ratios	1.148:1 constant mesh. 2.35:1 low ratio
Propeller shafts	Open drive. Hotchkiss type
Axles	Front - spiral bevel. Rear - spiral bevel or hypoid bevel gear, according to model of vehicle. Ratio 4.7:1
Differential	Two. One for each front and rear axles.

Overall ratios

	High gear	Low gear
1st	20.14:1	41.24:1
2nd	12.00:1	24.60:1
3rd	8.05:1	16.50:1
4th	5.40:1	11.10:1
Rev.	21.01:1	42.93:1

Transmission No. 2

Clutch	Single dry plate. Diaphragm spring
Clutch diameter	266 mm (10.5 in)
Main gearbox type	4 speed transmission synchromesh. 4 forward: 1 reverse speed. Synchromesh on forward speeds.
Main gearbox ratios	4.05:1 1st; 2.41:1 2nd; 1.61:1 3rd; 1.61:1 4th; 4.22:1 rev.
Transfer gearbox	2 speed reduction. On main gearbox output. 2/4 wheel drive control on transfer gearbox output
Transfer gearbox ratios	1.174:1 constant mesh. 3.32:1 low gear.
Propeller shafts	Open drive. Hotchkiss type.
Axles	Front - hypoid bevel gear. Fully floating. Rear same. Ratio 5.57:1
Differentials	Three, One in front and rear axles: one in transfer gearbox

Overall ratios

	High gear	Low gear
1st	26.48:1	74.88:1
2nd	15.76:1	44.57:1
3rd	10.53:1	29.78:1
4th	6.54:1	18.50:1
Rev	27.60:1	78.04:1

Transmission No. 3

This transmission is similar to No. 1, except for the front and rear axle ratio which affects the overall ratios

Axles	Front & rear - spiral bevel gear. Ratio 5.32:1
Differentials	Two. Front & rear axles

Overall ratios

	High gear	Low gear
1st	22.80:1	46.68:1
2nd	13.60:1	27.84:1
3rd	9.12:1	18.67:1
4th	6.11:1	12.50:1
Rev	23.73:1	48.58:1

TRUCK SPECIFICATIONS

Truck No. 1   Normal control
    ¼ ton cargo 4 x 4

Based on the then current specification of the Land Rover 2.23 metre (88 inch) wheelbase regular model. Changes to the specification have been made to render the vehicle more acceptable for Service use. The vehicle is capable of carrying 408 kgs (900 lb) of cargo across country in addition to the drive and one passenger. Mounting points are provided to accept wireless installation in an emergency.

Introduced in 1958. Still in service.

SPECIFICATION

Height	1.96 metres (77 inches)
Width	1.69 metres (66.5 inches)
Length	3.78 metres (149 inches)
Wheelbase	2.235 metres (88 inches)

Front & rear track
            1.308 metres (51.5 in.)
Unladen weight 1,462 Kgs (3,220 lb)
Laden weight   2,025 Kgs (4,460 lb)

PERFORMANCE

Speed (average maximum) road work
            72.42 km/hr (45 m.p.h.)
Speed (average maximum) cross country
            10.31 km/hr (12 m.p.h.)
Gross power weight ratio
            25.43 kW/t (34.67 bhp/t)

Maximum tractive effort, low gear
            9192 N/t (2,121 lb/Ton)
Maximum climbing ability
            40%
Maximum gradient for stop & restart
            37%
Range of action at average max speed
            450 km (280 miles)

TECHNICAL DATA

Power Unit -
Type   Rover 2.286 litre 4 cylinder in-line (petrol) gasoline. See Engine No.1 specification

Fuel System -
Type of fuel   Gasoline (petrol)
Air cleaner   Oil bath + pre-cleaner
Fuel capacity (twin tanks)
            90.86 litres (20 gall)

Engine Cooling -
System   Pressurised.Thermo-syphon

Wheels & Tyres -
Wheels & rims   4.50E x 16 W.D.divided pattern disc (FV84919)
Tyres, size   6.50 x 16 cross country tread pattern. 6 ply

Transmission -
Type (including the clutch)
            4 speed transmission. Synchromesh. See Transmission No. 1 spec.

Brakes -
Type   Hydraulic. Drum type.
Brake shoe diameter
            254 mm (10 inches)
Brake shoe width
            38 mm (1.5 inches)
Parking or hand brake
            Mechanical.On transmission
Brake drum diameter 228.6 mm (9 in.)
Brake shoe width   44.5 mm (1.75 44.5mm (1.75 in.)

Suspension -
Front & rear   Semi-elliptic longitudinal leaf spring.
Shock absorbers Double acting hydraulic telescopic front & rear

Electrical Equipment -
Generator or alternator
                    Generator - 12 volt D.C.
Batteries   12 volt (lead acid) 51
                    amp hour capacity
Suppression   F.V.R.D.E. spec. 2051.
                    Appendix D1.Schedule B
Body -
Length   1.14 metres (45.25 in.)
Width   1.42 metres (55.75 in.)
Sides (height) 0.508 metres (20 in.)
Steering -
Type   Recirculating ball type.
                    Worm and nut
Turning circle 12.8 metres (504 inches)
Towing Attachment -
Front   Provision only
Rear   Rotating/lockable   hook
                    (FV332151)
Variants -
Emergency wireless carrier (without
battery charging facilities).
Emergency stretcher carrier.
WOMBAT carrier
Line layer.
3.5 KVA Onan generator.
Helicopter & light aircraft slave start.
Electronics installation, requiring 24
volt power supply.

TRUCK No. 2   Normal control
    ¼ ton F F R 4 x 4

Based on the current specification of
the Land Rover 2.23 metre (88 inch)
wheelbase regular model. This vehicle is
similar to Truck No. 1, except for being
fitted with 24 volt electrical system
for radio. Classified as 'fitted for
radio' (F F R) version.
Introduced in 1958. Still in service.
SPECIFICATION
The dimensions are the same as for Truck
No. 1, except the weights vary -
Unladen weight 1,665 Kgs (3,668 lb)
inclusive of wireless fittings
Laden weight   2,163 Kgs (4,765 lb)
PERFORMANCE
Speed (average maximum) road work
                    72.44 km/hr (45 m.p.h.)
Speed (average maximum) cross country
                    19.31 km/hr (12 m.p.h.)
Gross power weight ratio
                    23.8 kW/t (32.4 bhp/T)
Maximum tractive effort, low gear
                    8786.4 N/t (2,014 lb/Ton)
Maximum climbing ability
                    38%
Maximum gradient for stop & restart
                    35%
Range of action at average max speed
                    563 km (350 miles)
TECHNICAL DATA
Similar to Truck No. 1, with the
exception of the following electrical
equipment and variants:
Electrical Equipment -
Generator or alternator
                    Generator - 24 volt A.C.
                    40 amp rectified
Batteries (vehicle) 2 x 12 volt 43 amp
                    hour (lead acid)
    (Equipment)   2 x 12 volt 100 amp hour
                    (lead acid)
Suppression   F.V.R.D.E. spec 2051.
                    Appendix D1. Schedule A
NOTE: Provision is made to charge
wireless batteries. Built-in equipment
for radio role - including wireless
table, battery carrier and 2 batteries

co-axial aerial leads, operator's table, etc.
Variants -
Helicopter & light aircraft starting. Electronics installation, requiring 24 volt power supply.

TRUCK No. 3   Normal control
¾ ton cargo 4 x 4

Based on the current specification of the Land Rover 2.77 metre (109 inch) wheelbase. Changes to the specification have been made to render it more acceptable to military service use. The vehicle is capable of carrying 762 kgs (1,680 lb) of cargo across country, in addition to the driver and one passenger Mounting points are provided to accept wireless equipment in an emergency. Introduced in 1958. Still in service.

SPECIFICATION

Height	1.98 metres (78 inches)
Width	1.66 metres (65.5 inches)
Length	4.65 metres (183 inches)
Wheelbase	2.77 metres (109 inches)

Front & rear tracks
       1.308 metres (51.5 in.)
Unladen weight 1,652 kgs (3,640 lb)
Laden weight   2,593 kgs (5,712 lb)
PERFORMANCE
Speed (average maximum) road work
       72.42 km/hr (45 m.p.h.)
Speed (average maximum) cross country
       16.09 km/hr (10 m.p.h.)

Gross power weight ratio
       19.86 kW/t (27.06 lb/Ton)
Maximum tractive effort, low gear
       6,717 N/t (1,540 lb/T)
Maximum climbing ability
       29%
Maximum gradient for stop & restart
       26%
Range of action at average max speed
       450 km (280 miles)

TECHNICAL DATA

Power Unit -
Type   Rover 2.286 litre 4 cylinder in line (petrol) gasoline. See Engine No.1 specification

Fuel System -
Type of fuel   Gasoline (petrol)
Air cleaner   Oil bath + pre-cleaner
Fuel capacity (twin tanks)
       90.86 litres (20 gall)

Engine Cooling -
System   Pressurised.Thermo-syphon

Wheels & Tyres -
Wheels & rims 5.50E x 16 W.D. Divided pattern disc (FV84930)
Tyres, size   7.50 x 16 cross country tread pattern. 6 ply

Transmission -
Type (including the clutch)
       4 speed transmission. Synchromesh. See Transmission No. 1 spec.

Brakes -
Type   Hydraulic. Drum type
Brake disc diameter
       279.4 mm (11 inches)
Brake shoe width
       57.15 mm (2.25 inches)
Parking or hand brake
       Mechanical.On transmission
 Brake drum diameter   228.6 mm (9 in.)
 Brake shoe width   44.5 mm (1.75 in)
Suspension -
Front & rear   Semi-elliptic longitudinal leaf springs

Shock absorbers

	Double acting hydraulic telescopic front & rear

Electrical Equipment -
Generator or alternator
    Generator. 12 volt D.C.
Batteries   12 volt (lead acid) 51 amp hour capacity
Suppression   F.V.R.D.E. spec 2051 Appendix D1. Schedule B
Body -
Length   1.85 metres (72.75 in.)
Width   1.44 metres (56.87 in.)
Sides (height) 0.483 metres (19 inches)
Steering -
Type   Recirculating ball type Worm and nut
Turning circle 15.24 metres (600 in.)
Towing Attachment -
Front   Provision only
Rear   Rotating/lockable hook (FV332151)
Variants -
Emergency wireless carrier (without battery charging facilities).
Emergency stretcher carrier.
WOMBAT carrier.

TRUCK No. 4   Normal control
    ¾ ton F F R 4 x 4

Based on the current specification of the Land Rover 2.77 metre (109 inch) wheelbase. This model is similar to Truck No. 3, except for being equipped with 24 volt electrical system for **radio** Classified as 'Fitted for radio' (F F **R**) Introduced in 1958. Still in service.
SPECIFICATION
The dimensions are similar to Truck **No.3** except -
Unladen weight (including radio fitting)
    1,843 kgs (4,060 lb)
Laden weight   2,542 kgs (5,600 lb)
PERFORMANCE
Speed (average maximum) road work
    72.42 km/hr (45 m.p.h.)
Speed (average maximum) cross country
    16.09 km/hr (10 m.p.h.)
Gross power weight ratio
    20.3 kW/t (27.6 bhp/Ton)
Maximum tractive effort, low gear
    6852 N/t (1,573 lb/Ton)
Maximum climbing ability
    29.5%
Maximum gradient for stop & restart
    26.5%
Range of action at average max speed
    450 km (280 miles)
TECHNICAL DATA
Same as for Truck No. 3, with the exception of the following electrical equipment -
Generator or alternator
    Generator - 24 volt A.C. 40 amp rectified
Batteries
  (Vehicle)   2 x 12 volt. 43 amp hour (lead acid)
  (Equipment)   2 x 12 volt. 100 amp hour (lead acid)
Suppression   F.V.R.D.E. spec. 2051 Appendix D1. Schedule A
NOTE: Provision is made to charge wireless batteries. Built-in equipment for radio role, including wireless table, battery carrier and 2 batteries, co-axial aerial leads, 2 operators' seats, H.F.aerial brackets, etc.
Variants -
Helicopter & light aircraft slave start.
Electronics installation, requiring 24 volt power supply.

TRUCK No. 5   Normal control
¾ ton airfield crash rescue
              4 x 4

This vehicle was developed to meet the
requirements of the Air Ministry for a
machine for immediate rescue from
crashed aircraft, to deal with aircraft
wheel brake fires, and to act as a light
auxiliary truck to escort aircraft to
dispersals. The vehicle is based on the
current specification of the Land Rover
2.77 metre (109 inch) wheelbase. Changes
have been made to render the vehicle
more acceptable to military service use.
Introduced in 1960. Still in service.
SPECIFICATION
Height   2.51 metres (99 inches)
Width   1.71 metres (67.5 inches)
Length   4.65 metres (183 in.)
Wheelbase   2.77 metres (109 inches)
Front & rear track
                1.308 metres (51.5 in.)
Unladen weight 2,270 kgs (5,000 lb)
Laden weight   2,631 kgs (5,796 lb)
PERFORMANCE
Speed (average maximum) road work
                72.42 km/hr (45 m.p.h.)
Speed (average maximum) cross country
                24 km/hr (15 m.p.h.)
Gross power weight ratio
                19.57 kW/t (26.7 bhp/T)
Maximum tractive effort, low gear
                6620.5 N/t (1,520 lb/Ton)

Maximum climbing ability
                28%
Maximum gradient for stop & restart
                25%
Range of action at average max speed
                225 km (140 miles)
TECHNICAL DATA
Power Unit -
Type   Rover   2.286   litre   4
                cylinder in line (petrol)
                gasoline. See Engine No.1
                specification
Fuel System -
Type of fuel   Gasoline (petrol)
Air cleaner   Oil bath + pre-cleaner
Fuel capacity   45.5 litres (10 gallons)
Engine Cooling -
System   Pressurised.Thermo-syphon
Wheels & Tyres -
Wheels & rims   5.50E x 16 W.D. divided
                pattern disc (FV84930)
Tyres, size   7.50 x 16 cross country
                tread pattern. 6 ply
Tyre pump   Mechanical
Chains   Commercial standard
Transmission -
Type   4 speed transmission. See
                Transmission No. 1 spec.
Brakes -
Type   Hydraulic. Drum type
Brake drum diameter
                279.4 mm (11 inches)
Brake shoe width
                57.15 mm (2.25 inches)
Parking or hand brake
                Mechanical.On transmission
Brake drum diameter   228.6 mm (9 in.)
Brake shoe width   44.5 mm (1.75 in)
Suspension -
Front & rear   Semi-elliptic longitudinal
                leaf springs
Shock absorber Double acting hydraulic
                telescopic front & rear
NOTE: The suspension was modified from
the standard to give an improved ride
and handling. The system remained the
same.

Electrical Equipment –
Generator or alternator
            Generator – 12 volt D.C.
Batteries   12 volt (lead acid) 51
            amp hour capacity
Suppression F.V.R.D.E.spec. 2051.
            Appendix D1. Schedule B
Body –
Dimensions as for Truck No. 3
Towing Attachment –
Front   Provision only
Rear   Special jaws & pin type
Special Equipment –
The fire fighting equipment includes –
 2 high pressure dry powder chemical
 extinguishers with discharge hose and
 nozzles.
 Ladder.
 Saws – hand & compressed air operated.
 Asbestos blanket & gloves.
Other equipment –
 FV pattern brush guard to protect the
 front of the vehicle.
 Heavy duty front bumper.
 High powered searchlight.
 Site illumination lamp.
 Safety harness for crew members.

TRUCK No. 6   Normal control
 Ambulance 2 stretcher 4 x 4

This vehicle has been designed to meet the requirements of the War Office, for a small ambulance for the evacuation of casualties from forward areas, offering greater comfort than stretcher kits previously carried in Jeep-type vehicles. The chassis is based on the commercial specification for the Land Rover 2.77 metres (109 inches) wheelbase station wagon. Changes have been made to the specifications to make the vehicle more acceptable for military service use.
Accommodation is offered for the medical attendant and 2 stretcher cases or, alternatively, one stretcher case and 3 sitting patients or, second alternative, six sitting patients.
Introduced in 1960. No longer in service

SPECIFICATION
Height   2.146 metres (84.5 in.)
Width   1.905 metres (75 in.)
Length   4.826 metres (190 in.)
Wheelbase   2.77 metres (109 in.)
Front & rear track
                    1.308 metres (51.5 in.)
Unladen weight 1,881 kgs (4,144 lb)
Laden weight   2,542 kgs (5,600 lb)
PERFORMANCE
Speed (average maximum) road work
                    72.42 km/hr (45 m.p.h.)
Speed (average maximum) cross country
                    24 km/hr (15 m.p.h.)
Gross power weight ratio
                    20.3 kW/t (27.6 bhp/T)
Maximum tractive effort, low gear
                    6852 N/t (1,573 lb/Ton)
Maximum climbing ability
                    29.5%
Maximum gradient for stop & restart
                    26.5%
Range of action at average max speed
                    450 km (280 miles)

TECHNICAL DATA
Power Unit -

Type	Rover 2.286 litres 4 cylinder in line gasoline (petrol).See Engine No. 1 spec.

Fuel System -

Type of fuel	Gasoline (petrol)
Air cleaner	Oil bath + pre-cleaner
Fuel capacity	(twin tanks) 90.86 litres (20 gall)

Engine Cooling

System	Pressurised. Thermo-syphon

Wheels & Tyres -

Wheels & rims	5.50E x 16 W.D.divided pattern disc (FV84930)
Tyres, size	7.50 x 16 cross country tread pattern. 6 ply light truck type.

Transmission -
Type (including clutch)

4 speed transmission. Synchromesh. See Transmission No. 1 spec.

Brakes -

Type	Hydraulic. Drum type
Brake drum diameter	279.4 mm (11 inches)
Brake shoe width	57.15 mm (2.25 inches)
Parking or hand brake	Mechanical. On transmission.
Brake drum diameter	228.6 mm (9in.)
Brake shoe width	44.5 mm (1.75in.)

Suspension -

Front & rear	Semi-elliptic longitudinal leaf springs
Shock absorbers	Double acting hydraulic telescopic front & rear

NOTE: The standard suspension was modified to give an improved ride and better handling characteristics. The system remained as leaf springs.

Electrical Equipment -
Generator or alternator

	Generator - 12 volt DC
Batteries	12 volt 51 amp hour capacity (lead acid)
Suppression	F.V.R.D.E. Spec. 2051. Appendix D1.Schedule B

Body -

Length, width.	Not available
Sides (height)	Not applicable

NOTE: the body is framed and panelled in aluminium and is thermally insulated. Cab & Body ventilation heating is provided.

Steering -

Type	Recirculating ball type Worm and nut

Turning circle 15.25 metres (600 in.)
Towing Attachment

	None
Variants -	None

TRUCK No 7   Normal control
Airportable. General purpose
1 ton (Scheme A) 4 x 4

This vehicle was designed to achieve minimum bulk for air transport; up to 3 vehicles can be stacked one on top of the other. It can be used with flotation kit (as shown on No.8 vehicle specification). It is based on the 2.77 metre (109 inch) wheelbase Land Rover chassis.

A special body was provided, capable of carrying either a driver and 8 fully equipped troops or a driver and one ton of stores on a flat platform.
Introduced in 1960. No longer in service

SPECIFICATION

Height	2.13 metres (84 inches)
Width	1.8 metres (71 inches)
Length	4.19 metres (165 in.)
Wheelbase	2.77 metres (109 in.)
Front & rear track	1.36 metres (53.5 in.)
Unladen weight	1,856 kgs (4,088 lb)
Laden weight	2,972 kgs (6,548 lb)

PERFORMANCE

Speed (average maximum) road work
72.42 km/hr (45 m.p.h.)
Speed (average maximum) cross country
24 km/hr (15 m.p.h.)
Gross power weight ratio
17.34 kW/t (23.6 lb/T)
Maximum tractive effort, low gear
6033 N/t (1,374 lb/Ton)
Maximum climbing ability
26%
Maximum gradient for stop & restart
23%
Range of action at average max speed
402 km (250 miles)

TECHNICAL DATA

Power Unit –
Type   Rover 2.286 litre 4 cylinder in line gasoline (petrol). See Engine No. 1 spec.
Fuel System –
Type of fuel   Gasoline (petrol)
Air cleaner   Oil bath + pre-cleaner
Fuel capacity (twin tanks)
90.86 litres (20 gall)
Engine Cooling –
System –   Pressurised. Thermo-syphon.
Wheels & Tyres –
Wheels & rims 6.50L x 16 well base commercial rims & disc

Tyres, size   9.00 x 16 cross country tread pattern. 6 ply
Transmission –
Type (including clutch)
4 speed transmission. Synchromesh. See Transmission No 3 spec.
Brakes –
Type   Hydraulic. Drum type
Brake drum diameter
279.4 mm (11 inches)
Brake shoe width
57.15 mm (2.25 inches)
Parking or hand brake
Mechanical. On transmission
Brake drum diameter
228.6 mm (9 inches)
Brake shoe width
44.5 mm (1.75 inches)
Suspension –
Front & rear   Semi-elliptic longi-tudinal leaf spring
Shock absorbers
Double acting hydraulic telescopic front & rear
Electrical Equipment –
Generator or alternator
Generator 24 volt AC
Batteries   24 volt (2 x 12) (lead acid) 43 amp hour cap.
Suppression   F.V.R.D.E. spec. 2051 Appendix D1.Schedule B
Equipment   24 volt rectified AC generating system to give power for tools & equipment
Body –
Length   1.85 metres (72.75 in.)
Width   1.44 metres (56.5 in.)
Sides (height) Not applicable
Steering –
Type   Recirculating ball type Worm and nut
Turning circle 15.25 metres (600 in.)

Towing –
Attachment   Front: provision only
                Rear: rotating/lockable
                hook (FV 332151)
Variants   None

TRUCK No. 8   Normal control
 Airportable. General purpose
      1 ton (Scheme A)
  with flotation kit. 4 x 4

This vehicle is the same as No. 7, but
fitted with floation kit, which com-
prises four rubberised fabric air bags
inflated by the vehicle's exhaust
system. Each bag is supported by a light
alloy framework that can quickly be
dismantled for stowage on the vehicle.
Water propulsion is provided by a
propeller mounted on the driving shaft
to the rear axle, aided by the rotation
of the rear wheels.
Introduced in 1960. No longer in service
SPECIFICATION
Height   2.13 metres (84 inches)
Width   3.4 metres (134 inches)
Length   6.65 metres (262 in.)
Wheelbase   2.77 metres (109 in.)
Front & rear track
              1.308 metres (51.5 in.)
Weight (unladen)
              1,932 kgs (4,255 lb)
Weight (laden) 3,050 kgs (6,719 lb)
PERFORMANCE
This is related to the vehicle only and
is the same as for Truck No. 7
TECHNICAL DATA
Unchanged to that for Truck No. 7

TRUCK No. 9   Normal control
 Cargo (Multifuel power unit)
      4 x 4

This vehicle was a standard 2.23 metre
(88 inch) wheelbase Land Rover, fitted
with a 2.53 litre (154.4 cu.in.) multi-
fuel engine, developed to satisfy the
War Office policy in respect of vehicle
power units.
The vehicle shown above was undergoing
performance assessment trials at the
F.V.R.D.E. in 1962.Not put into service
SPECIFICATION
Height   1.905 metres (75 in.)
Width   1.664 metres (65.5 in.)
Length   3.607 metres (142 in.)
Wheelbase   2.23 metres (88 in.)
Front & rear track
              1.308 metres (51.5 in.)
Unladen weight 1,468 kgs (3,235 lb)
Laden weight 2,072 kgs (4,565 lb)
PERFORMANCE
Speed (average maximum) road work
              72.42 km/hr (45 m.p.h.)
Speed (average maximum) cross country
              24 km/hr (15 m.p.h.)
Gross power weight ratio
              22.6 kW/t (30.9 bhp/T)
Maximum tractive effort, low gear
              15193 N/t (3,482 lb/T)
Maximum climbing ability
              62%

31

Maximum gradient for stop & restart
  59%
Range of action at average max speed
  450 km (280 miles)

TECHNICAL DATA
Power Unit
Type   Rover 2.53 litre 4
                cylinder multifuel. See
                Engine No.4 spec.
Fuel System -
Type of fuel   Diesel or gasoline
Air cleaner   Oil bath + pre-cleaner
Fuel capacity   45.5 litres (10 gall)
Engine Cooling -
System   Thermo-syphon. Press-
                urised.
Wheels & Tyres -
Wheels & rims   4.50E x 16 well base
                commercial type rim and
                disc
Tyres, size   6.50 x 16 cross country
                tread pattern. 6 ply
Transmission -
Type (including clutch)
                4 speed transmission.
                Synchromesh. See Trans-
                mission No.1 spec.

Brakes -
Type   Hydraulic. Drum type
Brake drum diameter
                254 mm (10 inches)
Brake shoe width
                38 mm (1.5 inches)
Parking or hand brake
                Mechanical. On trans-
                mission.
  Brake drum diameter   228.6mm (9 in.)
  Brake shoe width   44.5 mm (1.75 in)
Suspension -
Front & rear   Semi-elliptic longi-
                tudinal leaf springs
Shock absorbers
                Double acting hydraulic
                telescopic front & rear
Electrical Equipment -
Generator or alternator
                Generator - 12 volt DC

Batteries   12 volt (lead acid) 51
                amp hour capacity
Suppression   F.V.R.D.E. spec. 2051
                Appendix D1. Schedule B
Body -
Length   1.15 metres (45.25 in.)
Width   1.42 metres (55.75 in.)
Sides (height) 0.51 metres (20 inches)
Steering -
Type   Recirculating ball type
                Worm and nut
Turning circle 12.8 metres (504 in.)
Towing -
Attachment   Front: provision only
                Rear: rotating/lockable
                hook (FV 332151)
Variants   None

TRUCK No. 10   Normal control
Airportable. General purpose
  1 ton (Scheme B) 4 x 4

This vehicle, shown in the photograph
above, is a 'mock-up' in the design
stage in 1962, aimed at satisfying a
similar requirement for the military to
that of the airportable vehicle of
Scheme A (No. 7 & 8 vehicles).
Land Rover mechanical components were
proposed, but the body structure was to
be of exoskeletal form to provide
inherent flotation and made of fibre
glass formed plastic reinforced construction. A forward position was

provided for both driver and passenger
Introduced for consideration in 1961.
Not carried forward for the future.
SPECIFICATION
Height   2.13 metres (84 inches)
Width   1.83 metres (72 inches)
Length   4.27 metres (168 in.)
Wheelbase   2.46 metres (97 inches)
Front & rear track
                1.36 metres (53.5 in.)
Unladen weight 1,588 kgs (3,499 lb)
Laden weight   2,605 kgs (5,739 lb)
PERFORMANCE
Speed (average maximum) road work
                72.42 km/hr (45 m.p.h.)
Speed (average maximum) cross country
                24 km/hr (15 m.p.h.)
Gross weight power ratio
                19.7 kW/t (26.93 bhp/T)
Maximum tractive effort, low gear
                6867 N/t (1,575 lb/Ton)
Maximum climbing ability
                29.5%
Maximum gradient for stop & restart
                26.5%
Range of action at average max speed
                443 km (275 miles)
TECHNICAL DATA
Power Unit
Type   Rover 2.286 litre 4
                cylinder in line
                gasoline (petrol). See
                Engine No 1 spec.
Fuel System -
Type of fuel   Gasoline (petrol)
Air cleaner   Oil bath + pre-cleaner
Fuel capacity (twin tanks)
                90.86 litres (20 galls)
Engine Cooling -
System   Pressurised
                Thermo-syphon
Wheels & Tyres -
Wheels & rims   6.50L x 16 well base
                commercial rim & disc
Tyres, size   9.00 x 16 cross country
                tread pattern, light-
                weight. 6 ply rating

Transmission -
Type (including clutch)
                4 speed transmission.
                Synchromesh. See Trans-
                mission No. 3 spec.
Brakes -
Type   Hydraulic. Drum type
Brake drum diameter
                279.4 mm (11 inches)
Brake shoe width
                57.15 mm (2.25 inches)
Parking or hand brake Mechanical. On
                transmission.
Brake drum diameter
                228.6 mm (9 inches)
Brake shoe width
                44.5 mm (1.75 inches)
Suspension -
Front & rear   Semi-elliptic longi-
                tudinal leaf springs
Shock absorbers   Double acting
                hydraulic telescopic
                front & rear
Electrical Equipment -
Generator or alternator
                Generator - 12 volt DC
Batteries   12 volt (lead acid) 51
                amp hour capacity
Suppression   F.V.R.D.E. spec 2051.
                Appendix D1. Schedule B
Body-
Length   4.27 metres (168 in.)
Width   1.83 metres (72 inches)
Sides (height) Not applicable
Steering -
Type   Recirculating ball type
                Worm and nut
Turning circle Not available
Towing Attachment
                None
Variants -   None

TRUCK No. 11   Normal control
        Service vehicle
        for F.V.R.D.E. use
        Prototype only

This vehicle was a standard commercial 2.77 metre (109 inch) wheelbase Land Rover, fitted with a hard-top cab and a 2.286 litre diesel engine. Wakefield lubrication equipment was mounted on the vehicle, complete with a compressor. The vehicle was used to service military Land Rovers in the field.
Introduced in 1961. May still be used.
SPECIFICATION

Height	1.93 metres (76 inches)
Width	1.66 metres (65.5 in.)
Length	4.44 metres (175 in.)
Wheelbase	2.77 metres (109 in.)
Front & rear tracks	
	1.308 metres (51.5 in.)
Unladen weight	Not available
Laden weight	2,542 kgs (5,600 lb)

PERFORMANCE
Speed (average maximum) road work
            72.42 km/hr (45 m.p.h.)
Speed (average maximum) cross country
            24 km/hr (15 m.p.h.)
Gross power weight ratio
            16.5 kW/t (22.5 bhp/T)
Maximum tractive power, low gear
            5993 N/t (1,374 lb/Ton)
Maximum climbing ability
            25.6%
Maximum gradient for stop & restart
            22.6%
Range of action at average max speed
            450 km (280 miles)

TECHNICAL DATA
Power Unit -
Type   Rover 2.286 litres 4
                  cylinder in line diesel
                  See Engine No. 3 spec
Fuel System -
Type of fuel   Diesel (Derv)
Air cleaner   Oil bath + pre-cleaner
Fuel capacity   45.5 litres (10 gall)
Engine Cooling -
System   Pressurised. Thermo-syphon
Wheels & Tyres -
Wheels & rims   5.50E x 16 well base
                  commercial rims & discs
Tyres, size   7.50 x 16 cross country
                  tread pattern. 6 ply
Transmission -
Type (including clutch)
                  4 speed transmission.
                  Synchromesh. See Trans-
                  mission No. 1 spec.
Brakes -
Type   Hydraulic. Drum type
Brake drum diameter
                  270.4 mm (11 inches)
Brake shoe width
                  57.15 mm (2.25 inches)
Parking or hand brake Mechanical
                  On transmission
  Brake drum diameter
                  228.6 mm (9 inches)
  Brake shoe width
                  44.5 mm (1.75 inches)
Suspension -
Front & rear
                  Semi-elliptic longi-
                  tudinal leaf springs
Shock absorbers
                  Double acting hydraulic
                  telescopic front & rear
Electrical Equipment -
Generator or alternator
                  Generator - 12 volt DC
Batteries   12 volt (lead acid) 51
                  amp hour capacity
Suppression   F.V.R.D.E. spec 2051
                  Appendix D1. Schedule B

Body –
Length   1.85 metres (72.75 in.)
Width   1.44 metres (56.87 in.)
Sides (height) 0.48 metres (19 inches)
Steering –
Type   Recirculating ball type
                Worm and nut
Turning circle 15.25 metres (600 in.)
Towing –
Attachment   Front: provision only
                Rear: rotating/lockable
                hook (FV 332151)
Variants   None
Special Equipment –
Wakefield lubrication equipment, mounted on the vehicle, comprising – dispensers for grease, engine oil and two grades of gear oil. Also an attachment had been provided for a tyre inflation hose. A Clayton Dewandre twin cylinder air compressor capable of delivering 9 cubic feet/minute was provided in the equipment as a source of power.

TRUCK No. 12   Normal control
   $\frac{3}{4}$ ton general service/G.W.
              4 x 4

This vehicle was based on the $\frac{3}{4}$ ton Land Rover general service cargo vehicle, No. 3, but without any canvas tilt, canopy or side screens leaving the driver's compartment open to the weather. A folding windscreen was provided. The vehicle was fitted with a simple transversable launcher designed to fire Vigilant anti-tank missiles from the vehicle. Two missiles are in the ready-to-fire position in the above photograph.
Introduced in 1965. No longer in service, replaced by other missile launchers/carriers.
SPECIFICATION
Similar to Truck No. 3 ($\frac{3}{4}$ ton general service cargo model). Weights both laden and unladen are not available.
PERFORMANCE
Similar to Truck No. 3, but the tractive effort and gradability could depend upon the difference in weights between this version and that of Truck No. 3.
TECHNICAL DATA
Similar to that of Truck No. 3, but fitted with the following special equipment –
The launcher consists of a transversable centre section, with two missiles. This arrangement was mounted on a welded steel frame that carried three spare missiles. Further spare missiles may have been carried in the vehicle, aft of the drive and passengers. Firing could be carried out remote from the vehicle by using combined sight controller and separation cable.

TRUCK No. 13   Normal control
   $\frac{1}{2}$ ton general service (diesel)
              4 x 4

This vehicle was a 2.77 metre (109 inch) wheelbase Land Rover fitted with a hard top. It had a diesel engine with a flame trap and spark arrester, in lieu of a silencer. A 12 volt A.C. alternator had been substituted for the normal standard generator and there were changes to the electrical system to give power for the radio installation.

Introduced in 1959. No longer in service

SPECIFICATION

Similar to Truck No. 3, except –
Unladen weight 1,576 kgs (3,471 lb)
Laden weight   2,352 kgs (5,181 lb)

PERFORMANCE

Speed (average maximum) road work
          72.42 km/hr (45 m.p.h.)
Speed (average maximum) cross country
          24 km/hr (15 m.p.h.)
Gross power weight ratio
          21.52 kW/t (29.4 bhp/T)
Maximum tractive effort, low gear
          6568 N/t (1,506 lb/Ton)
Maximum climbing ability
          29%
Maximum gradient for stop & restart
          26%
Range of action at average max speed
          450 km (280 miles)

TECHNICAL DATA

Power Unit –
Type   Rover 2.286 litres 4
              cylinder diesel. See
              Engine No. 3 spec.

Fuel System –
Type of fuel Diesel (Derv)
Air cleaner   Oil bath + pre-cleaner
Fuel capacity 45.4 litres (10 gall)

Engine Cooling –
System   Pressurised. Thermo-syphon

Wheels & Tyres –
Wheels & rims 5.00 x 16 W.D. divided
              pattern disc
Tyres, size   7.00 x 16 cross country
              tread pattern. 6 ply

Transmission –
Type (including clutch)
              4 speed transmission.
              Synchromesh. See Trans-
              mission No. 1 spec.

Brakes –
Type   Hydraulic. Drum type
Brake drum diameter
              279.4 mm (11 inches)
Brake shoe width
              57.15 mm (2.25 inches)
Parking or hand   Mechanical on
              transmission
Brake drum diameter
              228.6 mm (9 inches)
Brake shoe width
              44.5 mm (1.75 inches)

Suspension –
Front & rear
              Semi-elliptic longi-
              tudinal leaf springs
Shock absorbers   Double acting
              hydraulic telescopic
              front & rear

Electrical Equipment –
Generator or alternator
              Alternator – 12 volt AC
              rectified
Batteries   12 volt (lead acid) 38
              amp hour capacity
Suppression   F.V.R.D.E. spec 2051
              Appendix D1. Schedule B

Body –
Length   1.85 metres (72.75 in.)
Width   1.44 metres (56.87 in.)
Sides (height) 0.48 metres (19 inches)

Steering –
Type   Recirculating ball type
              Worm and nut
Turning circle 14.32 metres (564 in.)

Towing –
Attachment   Front: single hook
              Rear: multi-hitch, 4
              position
Variants   None

TRUCK No. 14   Normal control
  General service. Line layer
          4 x 4

This vehicle is similar to the General
service vehicle No. 1, based on the Land
Rover 2.23 metres (88 inch) wheelbase
model. It has been modified to meet a
requirement for a light line layer
vehicle by fitting an applique kit of
parts developed by S.R.D.E.
Introduced in 1964. Still in service.
SPECIFICATION
Height (over structure only)
                2.31 metres (91 inches)
Width   1.73 metres (68 inches)
Length   3.79 metres (149 in.)
Wheelbase   2.23 metres (88 inches)
Front & rear tracks
                1.308 metres (51.5 in.)
Unladen weight (basic vehicle only)
                1,527 kgs (3,364 lb)
Laden weight   2,025 kgs (4,460 lb)
PERFORMANCE
Speed (average maximum) road work
                72.42 km/hr (45 m.p.h.)
Speed (average maximum) cross country
                19.3 km/hr (12 m.p.h.)
Gross power weight ratio
                25.3 kW/t (34.67 bhp/T)
Maximum tractive effort, low gear
                9086 N/t (2,121 lb/Ton)
Maximum climbing ability
                38%

Maximum gradient for stop & restart
                35%
Range of action at average max speed
                563 km (350 miles)
TECHNICAL DATA
Same as for the General service ¼ ton
Truck No. 1

TRUCK No. 15   Normal control
    Ambulance 2 & 4 stretcher
        ¾ ton 4 x 4

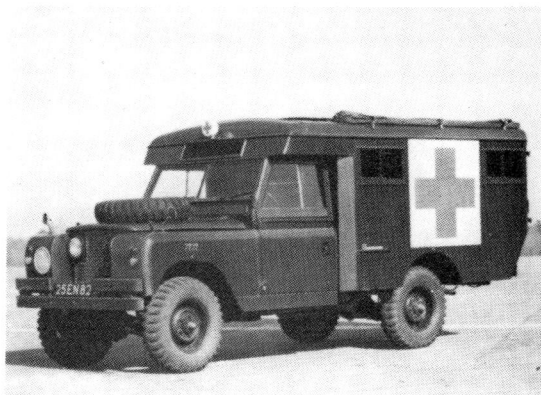

This model has been developed to meet
the requirements of the Ministry of
Defence (Army Department) for a small
ambulance suitable for evacuating
casualties from forward areas, offering
greater comfort than stretcher kits
previously carried in Jeep-type vehicles
Also could provide additional accommodation than the earlier ambulance
vehicle No. 6.
The chassis is based on the 2.77 metre
(109 inch) wheelbase Land Rover specifications. Changes were made to this
vehicle to make it more suitable for
service use. It offers accommodation for
a medical attendant and 2 or 4 stretcher
cases or, alternatively, one or two
stretcher cases and 3 sitting patients
or, a second alternative, 6 sitting
patients, all in addition to the driver.
Introduced in 1965. Still in service.

37

SPECIFICATION

Height	2.15 metres (84.5 in.)
Width	1.9 metres (75 inches)
Length	4.83 metres (190 in.)
Wheelbase	2.77 metres (109 in.)

Front & rear tracks
1.308 metres (51.5 in.)
Unladen weight 1.932 kgs (4,256 lb)
Laden weight 2,672 kgs (5,885 lb)

PERFORMANCE

Speed (average maximum) road work
72.42 km/hr (45 m.p.h.)
Speed (average maximum) cross country
16.09 km/hr (10 m.p.h.)
Gross power weight ratio
19.2 kW/t (26.24 bhp/T)
Maximum tractive effort, low gear
6519 N/t (1,495 lb/Ton)
Maximum climbing ability
29.5%
Maximum gradient for stop & restart
26.5%
Range of action at average max speed
450 km (280 miles)

TECHNICAL DATA

Similar to that of Truck No. 3 ($\frac{3}{4}$ ton F F R), except for improved leaf spring suspension to improve the ride and handling and the body –
Length & width Not available
Sides (height) Not applicable
Variants –
A similar ambulance model is used by the Ministry of Defence (Royal Air Force).

TRUCK No. 16   Normal control
$\frac{1}{4}$ ton general service
lightweight (stripped) 4 x 4

This vehicle was developed to meet a General Staff requirement for a light weight airportable, helicopter-liftable vehicle, with a useful payload and capable of towing light support weapons. The vehicle was based on the existing in-service truck $\frac{1}{4}$ ton chassis, having a power unit, transmission, suspension brakes and steering in common. The main differences between the vehicles was in respect of the body construction, which was designed to meet the same roles as the existing vehicle and offering a similar degree of weather protection. It was also capable of being reduced still further in weight and bulk to a greater extent for air transportation and helicopter lifting, resulting in a stark, but useful, vehicle weighing about 1,135 kgs (2,500 lb). The vehicle was capable of carrying a payload of 406 kgs (896 lb) plus driver and one passenger. It could be fitted with either 8.25 x 15 ribbed desert tread pattern tyres or 6.50 x 16 cross country tread pattern of 6 ply rating.
Introduced in 1965. No longer in service; replaced by a similar design, but of $\frac{1}{2}$ ton capacity.

SPECIFICATION
Height   1.47 metres (58 inches)
Width   1.52 metres (60 inches)
Length   3.63 metres (143 in.)
Wheelbase   2.23 metres (88 inches)
Front & rear tracks
                1.308 metres (51.5 in.)
Unladen weight (with full fuel)
                1,407 kgs (3,100 lb)
Laden weight   1,996 kgs (4,396 lb)
PERFORMANCE
Speed (average maximum) road work
                72.42 km/hr (45 m.p.h.)
Speed (average maximum) cross country
                19.31 km/hr (12 m.p.h.)
Gross power weight ratio
                26 kW/t (35 bhp/Ton)
Maximum tractive effort, low gear
                8608 N/t (1,976 lb/Ton)
Maximum climbing ability
                37%
Maximum gradient for stop & restart
                34%
Range of action at average max speed
                563 km(350 miles)
The above tractive effort and gradient
are calculated with 8.25 x 15 tyre
equipment.
TECHNICAL DATA
As for Truck No. 1, except –
Wheels & Tyres –
Wheels & rims   5.00F x 15 well base
                commercial rim & disc
                (for 8.25 x 15 tyres)
                5.00F x 16 well base
                commercial rim & disc
                (for 6.50 x 16 tyres)
Tyres, size   8.25 x 15 ribbed desert
                tread pattern; or 6.50
                x 16 cross country
                tread pattern
Tyre pump   Manual
Chains   Standard commercial
Suspension –
Front & rear   Semi-elliptic longi-
                tudinal leaf springs

Shock absorbers
                Double acting hydraulic
                telescopic front & rear
Body –
Length & width Not available
Sides (height) Not applicable
Variants –
Emergency wireless carrier (without
 battery charging facilities)
Emergency stretcher cases.

TRUCK No. 17   Normal control
   ¼ ton general service
     lightweight F F R

This vehicle was the radio equipment
carrying version with full tilt, side
screens and full windscreen of the No.
16 vehicle. Under development in 1966,
not in service.
SPECIFICATION
Height   1.96 metres (77 inches)
Width   1.62 metres (63.75 in.)
Length   3.73 metres (147 in.)
Wheelbase   2.23 metres (88 inches)
Front & rear tracks
                1.308 metres (51.5 in.)
Weight (unladen with full fuel tank &
wireless fittings, but no sets)
                1,596 kgs (3,514 lb)
Weight (laden) 1,995 kgs (4,396 lb)

PERFORMANCE

Speed (average maximum) for road and cross country work; Gross power weight ratio; and Range of action at average maximum speed As Truck No. 16
Maximum tractive effort, low gear
9380 N/t (2,150 lb/Ton)
Maximum climbing ability
41%
Maximum gradient for stop & restart
38%

TECHNICAL DATA

Similar to Truck No. 16, except –
Electrical Equipment –
Generator or alternator
Generator – 24 volt AC with built-in silicon diode rectifier (90 amp output)
Batteries
(vehicle)   2 x 12 volt (lead acid) 43 amp hour capacity
(equipment)   2 x 12 volt (lead acid) 100 amp hour capacity
Suppression   F.V.R.D.E. spec. 2051 Appendix D1. Schedule A
NOTE: Provision was made for a second pair of batteries where increased capacity was needed.
Body –
Length   3.65 metres (144 in.)
Width   1.52 metres (60 inches)
Sides (height) 0.5 metres (20 inches)
Variants –
None was contemplated at that time, but the development of this vehicle continued and it was replaced by a similar version of ½ ton general service machine.

TRUCK/TRAILER No. 18   Normal control
¾ ton cargo truck and
¾ ton trailer (power driven)

The 2.23 metre (88 inch) wheelbase Land Rover and axle driven Scottorn trailer are available commercially. The 2.77 metre (109 inch) wheelbase version and trailer were prototyped for technical assessment in aid of the Ministry of Defence (Royal Air Force) requirement for a light tactical airportable fire appliance and for research.
The basic vehicle was the ¾ ton general service F F R (as truck No. 4). An additional transfer gearbox at the rear of the vehicle was coupled to the vehicle's main gearbox and gave power to drive the coupled trailer, which was similar in description and specification to Trailer No. 1. The shaft coupling the trailer to the vehicle was of tubular design with single universal joints and was quickly detachable when the trailer was uncoupled.
Introduced in 1965. No longer in service

SPECIFICATION
(For vehicle train)
Height   2.06 metres (81 inches)
Width
(vehicle)   1.69 metres (66.5 in.)
(trailer)   1.8 metres (71 inches)
Length   7.52 metres (296 in.)
Unladen weight 2,226 kgs (4,903 lb)
Laden weight 3,994 kgs (8,796 lb)
PERFORMANCE
Speed (average maximum) road work
72.42 km/hr (45 m.p.h.)
Speed (average maximum) cross country
16.09 km/hr (10 m.p.h.)
Gross power weight ratio
12.9 kW/t (17.56 bhp/T)
Maximum tractive effort, low gear
4351 N/t (1,000.5 lb/T)
Maximum climbing ability
33%

Maximum gradient for stop & restart
30%
Range of action at average max speed
403 km (250 miles)
TECHNICAL DATA
Same as the ¾ ton F F R vehicle No. 4.
The Technical Data for the power driven
trailer is the same as Trailer No. 1.

TRUCK No. 19   Normal control
   ¾ ton cargo truck
 for power trailers - 4 x 4

This was a private venture by Land Rover
Company to provide a vehicle specially
for drawing power-driven trailers.
Similar in style to Truck No. 17, but
incorporating the following features -
 Increased power
  Power drive transfer gearbox for
trailed loads, allowing optional choice
of 6 x 6; 6 x 4; or 6 x 2 wheel drive
 Increased wheelbase to 2.8 metres (110
inches)
 Large diameter and section tyres
 Improved approach and departure angles
 Lightweight style body capable of being
stripped to reduce weight for airporting
operations.
Introduced in 1965. Never put into
service.

SPECIFICATION
Height   2.03 metres (80 inches)
Width   1.83 metres (72 inches)
Length   4.34 metres (171 in.)
Wheelbase   2.79 metres (110 in.)
Front & rear tracks
                1.51 metres (59.5 in.)
Unladen weight 1,725 kgs (3,800 lb)
Weight (stripped for airporting)
                1,498 kgs (3,300 lb)
Laden weight   2,951 kgs (6,500 lb)
Weight (gross train weight - truck and
trailer)   4,995 kgs (11,000 lb)
PERFORMANCE
Speed (average max.) road work (solo)
                80.4 km/hr (50 m.p.h.)
 Cross country (solo)
                40.3 km/hr (25 m.p.h.)
 Road work (with trailer)
                64.3 km/hr (40 m.p.h.)
 Cross country (with trailer)
                32.2 km/hr (20 m.p.h.)
Gross power weight ratio (solo)
                27.7 kW/t (38 bhp/Ton)
(with trailer)
                16.4 kW/t (22.4 bhp/T)
Maximum tractive effort, low gear
 (solo)   12,209 N/t (2,674 lb/T)
 (with trailer) 7,232 N/t (1,653 lb/T)
Maximum climbing ability
 (solo)   52.7%
 (with trailer)   31%
Maximum gradient for stop & restart
 (solo)   49.7%
 (with trailer)   28%
Range of action at average max speed
 (solo)   482.5 km (300 miles)
 (with trailer) 402.3 km (250 miles)

TECHNICAL DATA
Power Unit -
Type   Rover 2.995 litres. 6
                cylinder in line gasoline
                (petrol) See Engine No.5
Fuel System -
Type of fuel   Gasoline (petrol)
Air cleaner   Oil bath + pre-cleaner

Fuel capacity (twin fuel tanks)
90.86 litres (20 gall)

Engine Cooling -
System   Pressurised.Thermo-syphon

Wheels & Tyres -
Wheels & rims   6.50L x 16 well base
                commercial rims & discs
Tyres, size   9.00 x 16 cross country
                tread pattern. 6 ply
Chains   Provision for fitting
                front & rear

Transmission -
Type (including clutch)
                4 speed transmission
                Synchromesh. See Trans-
                mission No. 4 spec.

Brakes -
Type   Hydraulic. Drum type
Brake drum diameter   Not available
Brake shoe width   Not available
Parking or hand brake Mechanical. On
                transmission
Brake drum diameter   Not available
Brake shoe width   Not available
Trailer brake   Single line inverted
                vacuum cylinder,
                actuating hydraulic
                drum brakes.

Suspension -
Front & rear   Semi-elliptic longi-
                tudinal leaf springs
Shock absorbers Double acting hydraulic
                telescopic front & rear

Electrical Equipment -
Generator or alternator
                Generator - 12 volt DC,
                or Alternator - 24 volt
                90 amp
Batteries   One 12 volt, 9 plate or
                2 x 12 volt 9 plates
Suppression   F.V.R.D.E. spec. 2051.
                Appendix D1. Sch B or D

Body -

Height, Width, Sides   Not available

Steering -
Type   Recirculating ball type
                Worm and nut
Turning circle 14.32 metres (564 in.)

Towing -
Attachment   Front: standard hook
                Rear: articulated
                coupling, concentric
                with the drive line to
                the powered trailer,
                interchangeable with
                standard hook.

Variants   None

TRUCK No. 20   Forward control
      1 ton cargo 4 x 4

This vehicle was a commercial development based on the standard 2.77 metre
(109 inch) wheel base Land Rover of the
normal control type. The cab was moved
forward to a position over the front
axle and raised to achieve the necessary
clearance with the engine and the front
wheels. Heavy duty axles manufactured by
E.N.V.Ltd. had been fitted: these were
of wider track width, together with the
wider spacing of the springs compensated
for the higher centre of gravity of the
vehicle. It was powered by the Rover 4
cylinder 2.286 litre petrol engine, in
common with the Land Rover normal
control range. An alternative power unit
would be made available. The vehicle was
undergoing assessment by the F.V.R.D.E.

as a 1 ton load carrier in 1966.
Introduced in 1965. No longer in
service. Replaced by Truck No. 24.

SPECIFICATION

Height (cab)	2.25 metres (88.5 in.)
Height of canopy	2.54 metres (100 in.)
Width	1.8 metres (70.75 in.)
Length	5.07 metres (199.5 in.)
Wheelbase	2.8 metres (110 inches)
Front & rear track	1.46 metres (57.5 in.)
Unladen weight	2,034 kgs (4,480 lb)
Laden weight	3,232 kgs (7,120 lb)

PERFORMANCE

Speed (average maximum) road work
64.3 km/hr (40 m.p.h.)
Speed (average maximum) cross country
16.09 km/hr (10 m.p.h.)
Gross power weight ratio
15.9 kW/t (21.76 bhp/T)
Maximum tractive effort, low gear
6774 N/t (1,554 lb/Ton)
Maximum climbing ability
29%
Maximum gradient for stop & restart
26%
Range of action at average max speed
273 km (170 miles)

TECHNICAL DATA

Power Unit –
Type   Rover 2.286 litres 4
                cylinder in line
                gasoline (petrol). See
                Engine No. 1 spec.
Fuel System –
Type of fuel   Gasoline (petrol)
Air cleaner   Oil bath + pre-cleaner
Fuel capacity   77.3 litres (17 gall)
Engine Cooling Pressurised.Thermo-syphon
Wheels & Tyres –
Wheels & rims   6.50L x 16 well base
                commercial type rims &
                discs
Tyres, size   9.00 x 16 cross country
                tread pattern. 6 ply
Chains   Commercial pattern

Transmission –
Type (including clutch)   4 speed
                transmission. Synchro-
                mesh. See Transmission
                No. 5 spec.
Brakes –
Type   Hydraulic. Drum type
Brake drum diameter
                Not available
Brake shoe width   Not available
Parking or hand brake Mechanical. On
                transmission
Brake drum diameter & shoe width
                Not available
Suspension –
Front & back   Semi-elliptic longi-
                tudinal leaf springs
Shock absorbers   Double acting
                hydraulic telescopic
                front & rear
Electrical Equipment –
Generator or alternator
                Generator – 12 volt DC
Batteries   12 volt (lead acid) 51
                amp hour capacity
Suppression   F.V.R.D.E. spec. 2051
                Appendix D1. Schedule B
Body –
Length, width, height (sides)
                Not available
Steering –
Type   Recirculating ball type
                Worm and nut
Turning circle 15.25 metres (600 in.)
Towing –
Attachment   Front: nil
                Rear: rotating/lockable
                hook (FV 332151)
Variants –   Possibly an ambulance
                version

TRUCK No. 21   Forward control
    1½ ton cargo - 4 x 4

This vehicle was designed to meet a requirement for a general service 30 cwt load carrier. It was equipped with a diesel engine and four wheel drive. The front wheel drive selection was controlled by the driver and available in all gears. In production a general service or specialist body would be fitted. The load platform was suitable for carrying a 1 ton container.
Introduced in 1965. No longer in service
SPECIFICATION
Height   2.64 metres (104 in.)
Width   2.22 metres (87.25 in.)
Length   4.73 metres (186.5 in.)
Wheelbase   2.84 metres (112 in.)
Front & rear tracks
                167 metres (66 inches)
Unladen weight 3,386 kgs (7,460 lb)
Laden weight   4,926 kgs (10,850 lb)
PERFORMANCE
Speed (average maximum) road work
                64.3 km/hr (40 m.p.h.)
Speed (average maximum) cross country
                24 km/hr (15 m.p.h.)
Gross power weight ratio
                15.9 kW/t (21.6 bhp/T)
Maximum tractive effort, low gear
                11393 N/t (2,611 lb/Ton)
Maximum climbing ability
                48%

Maximum gradient for stop & restart
                45%
Range of action at average max speed
                676 km (420 miles)
TECHNICAL DATA
Power Unit -
Type   Perkins 6.354 diesel. 6
                cylinder in line
Capacity   5,800 cc (354 cu.in.)
Maximum power   78.33 kW (105 b.h.p.) @
                2,500 r.p.m.
Nett torque   329.5 Nm (243 lbft) @
                1,450 r.p.m.
Governed speed 2.500 r.p.m.
Ignition   Compression ignition
Fuel System -
Type   Pressurised. Constant
                flow
Type of fuel   Diesel (Derv)
Air cleaner   Oil bath
Fuel capacity   127.5 litres (28 gall)
Engine lubrication -
System   Wet sump.Fullforce feed
Engine Cooling -
                Pressurised. Thermo-syphon
Wheels & Tyres -
Wheels & rims   6.50 x 16 well base
                commercial rims & discs
Tyres, size   11.00 x 16 cross
                country tread pattern
Tyre pump   Inflator provided
Chains   Non-skid commercial
Transmission -
Clutch   Single dry plate
Clutch diameter Not available
Transmission (main gearbox)
                5 speed synchromesh. 5
                forward, 1 reverse
Gearbox ratios Not available
Transfer gearbox
                2 speed constant mesh
Transfer gearbox ratios
                1.0:1 constant mesh.
                2.105:1 low gear
Axles (f & r) Spiral bevel full float
Axle ratio   4.67:1
Overall ratios 4.67:1 high:74.55:1 low

44

Differentials   One in each axle f & r
Propeller shaft   Open drive shaft.
                Hotchkiss type
Brake -
Type   Hydraulic: air assisted
                Drum type
Brake drum diameter & shoe width
                Not available
Parking or hand brake
                Mechanical. On rear
                wheels
Trailer brake   Air brake system
Warning device Gauge
Suspension -
Front & rear   Semi-elliptic longi-
                tudinal leaf springs
Shock absorbers   Double acting
                hydraulic telescopic
Electrical Equipment -
Generator or alternator
                Generator - 24 volt. 90
                amp A C (A.C.90)
Batteries   2 x 12 volt. U.K. 6TN
Suppression   F.V.R.D.E. spec 2051.
                Appendix D1. Schedule B
Body -
Length, width, height (side)
                Not available
Steering -
Type   Recirculating ball type
                Worm and nut
Turning circle R.H.lock: 14.44 metres
                (569 inches)
                L.H.lock: 13.74 metres
                (541 inches)
Towing -
Attachment - Front & rear -Hook
Variants -   None

TRUCK No. 22   Forward control
      1 tonne general service
              4 x 4

This vehicle was designed to replace
Truck No. 20 after development. It was
to meet a requirement for a high power
to weight ratio, helicopter liftable,
general service 1 tonne (0.98 Tons) load
carrier. The body was fitted with hinged
removeable sides and tailgate and points
were provided for lashing loads or
modules. The 2.49 metre (98 inch) x
1.727 metre (68 inch) body allowed
maximum use of the vehicle for
specialist installations.
The vehicle can be supplied with the
following equipment -
 Rear seating for 8 personnel in full
kit.
 24 volt electrical system, fully
suppressed for radio.
 Side mounted, easily removeable, 1802
kg (3,969 lb) capstan with storage drum.
In service in 1980/81. Still in service
SPECIFICATION
Height   2.185 metres (86.02 in)
Width   1.842 metres (72.52 in)
Length   4.278 metres (168.5 in)
Wheelbase   2.794 metres (110 in.)
Front track   1.524 metres (60 in.)
Rear track   1.549 metres (61 in.)
Unladen weight 1,862 kgs (4,101.3lb)
Laden weight   3,654 kgs (8,048.3 lb)

PERFORMANCE
Speed (average maximum) road work
            100 km/hr (62.14 m.p.h)
Speed (average maximum) cross country
            Not available
Gross power weight ratio
            33.15 k/W (45.19 bhp/T)
Maximum tractive effort, low gear
            13009 N/t (2.963 lb/T)
Maximum climbing ability
            56%
Maximum gradient for stop & restart
            53%
Range of action at average max speed
            560 km (348 miles)
TECHNICAL DATA
Power Unit -
Type   Rover 3.5 litre 8
                cylinder. 'V' formation
                gasoline (petrol). See
                Engine No. 2 spec.
Fuel System -
Type of fuel   Gasoline (petrol)
Air cleaner   A.C.Cyclone
Fuel capacity   114 litres (25 gall)
Engine Cooling -
System   Pressurised.Thermo-syphon
Wheels & Tyres -
Wheels & rims   6.50L x 16 well base
                commercial rims & discs
Tyres, size   9.00 x 16 cross country
                tread pattern
Transmission -
Type (including clutch)
                4 speed transmission.
                Synchrosmesh. See
                Transmission No. 2 spec
Brakes -
Type   Hydraulic. Servo assisted.
                Drum type
Parking or hand brake
                Mechanical. On trans-
                mission
Suspension -
Front & rear   Semi-elliptic longi-
                tudinal taper leaf
                springs

Shock absorbers
                Double acting hydraulic
                telescopic front & rear
                Rubber buffers provided
Electrical Equipment -
Generator or alternator
                Alternator - Lucas 16
                ACR 12 volt
Batteries   12 volt 63 amp hour cap
Suppression   M.V.E.E.spec. 595.
                Appendix D. Schedule B
Body -
Length   2.49 metres (98 inches)
Width   1.727 metres (68 in.)
Sides (height) Not available
Steering -
Type   Recirculating ball type
                Worm and nut
Turning circle 11.3 metres (444.9 in.)
Towing -
Attachment   Front: none
                Rear: standard hook
Variants -   F F R 24 with or
                without hardtop

AMBULANCE No. 23   Forward control
    1 tonne 4 stretcher 4 x 4

This model was developed to meet the
requirements of GASR 2525/1 for an
ambulance variant of the Truck general
service 1 tonne Land Rover No. 22.
The body, which is mainly framed and
pannelled in aluminium, is thermally
insulated and offers accommodation for a
medical attendant and 2 or 4 stretcher
cases or, alternatively, 1 or 2 stretcher cases and a number of sitting
patients, or an attendant and 8 sitting
patients, in addition to the driver and
one passenger in the cab. Cab and body
ventilation and heating is provided, as
is a built-in oxygen supply for the
stretcher cases. The vehicle is fitted
with either compressed air/oxygen

46

resuscitation equipment facility or a cooled air supply, with outlets for each stretcher location. Additonal facilities are also available to meet Royal Air Force crash rescue requirements, which includes mains electricity input for engine pre-heating and battery trickle charging, radio installation, and stowages for 2 gas cylinders of nitrous oxide and oxygen mixture (ENTONOX).

Chassis components are common to the 1 tonne truck version with the exception of 'up-rated' shock absorbers and a higher output alternator with split charging system.

Introduced in 1980. Still in service.

SPECIFICATION

Height	2.52 metres (99.2 in.)
Width	2.13 metres (83.8 in.)
Length	4.394 metres (172.99in)
Wheelbase	2.794 metres (110 in.)
Front track	1.525 metres (60 in.)
Rear track	1.55 metres (61 inches)
Unladen weight	2,803 kgs (6,174 lb)
Laden weight	3,654 kgs (8,048 lb)

PERFORMANCE

As for Truck No. 22

TECHNICAL DATA

As for Truck No. 22, except for body, size and type.

Variants   None, except as listed above.

This was based on the specially strengthened 2.77 metre (109 inch) wheelbase Land Rover chassis, incorporating improved crew protection.

The hull and turret are of welded armour plate. Armament consists of 7.62mm (0.30 in.) Browning machine gun with turret-mounted smoke projector, if so desired. A later version, known as the Mark 4, was introduced in the late 70s with improvements and using the Rover 3.5 litre V8 petrol engine.

Introduced in 1962. Still in service.

SPECIFICATIONS

Height	2.29 metres (90 inches)
Width	1.78 metres (70 inches)
Length	4.6 metres (181 inches)
Wheelbase	2.77 metres (109 in.)
Front & rear tracks	1.36 metres (53.5 in.)
Unladen weight	2,815 kgs (6,200 lb)
Laden weight	3,133 kgs (6,900 lb)
Unladen weight - Mark 4 version	Not available
Laden weight - Mark 4 version	3,360 kgs (7,400 lb)

PERFORMANCE

Speed (average maximum) road work
80.47 km/hr (50 m.p.h.)

Speed (average maximum) cross country
            48.28 km/hr (30 m.p.h.)
Gross power weight ratio
            16.3 kW/t (22.4 bhp/T)
Maximum tractive effort, low gear
            7915 N/t (1,783 lb/Ton)
Maximum climbing ability
            21.3%
Maximum gradient for stop & restart
            18.3%
Range of action at average max speed
            Standard 322 km (200 m)
            Long range 644 km(400m)
PERFORMANCE (with Mark 4 version, with
3.5 litre V8 petrol engine)
Speed (average maximum) road work
            104.6 km/hr (65 m.p.h.)
Speed (average maximum) cross country
            64.3 km/hr (40 m.p.h.)
Gross power weight ratio
            36.0 kW/t (49.1 bhp/T)
Maximum tractive effort, low gear
            5194 N/t (1172 lb/T)
Maximum climbing ability
            59%
Maximum gradient for stop & restart
            56%
Range of action at average max speed
            Standard tanks 257 km (160 m)

            Long range tanks 514 km (320
            Long range tanks 514 km(320 m)
TECHNICAL DATA
Power Unit
Type   Rover 2.286 litre 4
                  cylinder in line
                  gasoline (petrol). See
                  Engine No. 1 spec.
Governed speed 4,100 r.p.m.
Power Unit (Mark 4 version) -
Type   Rover 3.528 litre 8
                  cylinder 'V' formation
                  gasoline (petrol). See
                  Engine No. 2 spec.
Fuel System -
Type of fuel   Gasoline (petrol)
Air cleaner   Oil bath + pre-cleaner

Fuel capacity (standard tanks)
            63.6 litres (14 gall)
Fuel capacity (Long range tanks)
            127.2 litres (28 gall)
Engine Cooling -
System   Pressurised.Thermo-syphon
Wheels & Tyres -
Wheels, rims   6.50L x 16 standard
                  commercial rims & discs
Tyes, size   9.00 x 16 cross country
                  tread pattern. 6 ply
Transmission -
Type (including clutch)
                  4 speed transmission.
                  Synchromesh. See Trans-
                  mission No. 1 spec,
                  except for front & rear
                  axles, which are E.N.V.
                  Ltd. type
Type (including clutch): Mark 4
                  4 speed transmission.
                  Synchromesh. See Trans-
                  mission No. 2 spec.
                  NOTE: both these trans-
                  fer gearboxes are
                  permanently in 4 wheel
                  drive with differential
                  lock
Brakes -
Type   Hydraulic. Drum type
            Mark 4 Servo assisted
Brake drum diameter
            279.4 mm (11 inches)
Brake shoe width
            57.14 mm (2.25 inches)
Parking or hand   Mechanical. On
            transmission.
  Brake drum diameter
            228.6 mm (9 inches)
  Brake shoe width
            44.5 mm (1.75 inches)
Suspension -
Front & rear   Semi-elliptic longi-
                  tudinal leaf springs
            Mark 4 Anti-roll bar fitted

Shock absorbers
Double acting hydraulic telescopic front & rear

Electrical Equipment –
Generator or alternator
Generator - Lucas C40/1
Mark 4   Alternator- 18ACR-45amp
Batteries   12 volt (lead acid) heavy duty type
Suppression   Limited suppression standard. Full suppression optional. Both F.V.R.D.E. spec 2051 or M.V.E.E.spec 595. Appendix D. Schedule B or A

Body –
Length   3.22 metres (126.8 in.)
Width   1.78 metres (70 inches)
Side (height) Not applicable

The body was built and supplied by Short Brothers, Belfast. The hull and turret are of welded steel armour plate. The turret seat is adjustable for height and the turret itself rotates through 360 degrees. Sighting of the armament is aided by an optical periscope. For night operation, a floodlight, mounted on the turret, is synchronised with the armament in azimuth and elevation. The vehicle's twin windscreens are protected by drop down armoured visors with laminated glass inserts to give good forward visibility. The fuel tank is enclosed in an armour plated boot and the filler cap is released from inside the vehicle.

Steering –
Type   Recirculating ball type worm and nut
Turning circle 17.75 metres (699 in.)

Towing –
Attachment   Twin hook front & rear

Variants –
A similar model, Armoured Personnel Vehicle, is available and used for Security Forces in high risk areas. The specifications are identical, except for the body shape. The A P V is in the shape of a van.

For comparison, the Austin Airlift project is illustrated below with specification. This vehicle, whilst tested, was not proceeded with. On first sight, it gives the impression of not having sufficient belly clearance for rough terrain

AUSTIN

TRUCK   Normal control
        Project state
   (Engineering model)
Light airportable 4 x 4

An experimental prototype designed and built by the British Motor Corporation (British Leyland) to meet a General Staff requirement for an airportable vehicle. It provided accommodation for a driver and 3 passengers or, alternatively, a driver and 363 kg (800 lb) of cargo

SPECIFICATION
Height   1.51 metres (59.5 in.)
Width   1.37 metres (54 inches)

Length	2.82 metres (111 in.)	Tyres, size	5.60 x 12 cross country tread pattern
Wheelbase	1.97 metres (77.4 in.)	Chains	Non-skid commercial
Front & rear tracks	1.2 metres (47.25 in.)	Transmission – Clutch	Single dry plate
Unladen weight	725 kgs (1,598 lb)	Clutch diameter	181 mm (7.12 inches)
Laden weight	1,180 kgs (2,598 lb)	Transmission main gearbox	4 speed synchromesh. 4 forward, 1 reverse

PERFORMANCE

Speed (average maximum) road work
64.36 km/hr (40 m.p.h.)

Speed (average maximum) cross country
19.3 km/hr (12 m.p.h.)

Gross power weight ratio
31.4 kW/t (43.1 bhp/T)

Maximum tractive effort, low gear
6517 N/t (1,468 lb/Ton)

Maximum climbing ability
66%

Maximum gradient stop & restart
50%

Range of action at average max speed
450 km (280 miles)

TECHNICAL DATA

Power Unit –

Type   B.M.C. (British Leyland) 1,100 litre 4 cylinder in-line gasoline (petrol)

Capacity   1,098 cc (67 cu.in.)

Maximum power   37.3 kW (50 b.h.p.) @ 5,000 r.p.m.

Nett torque   81.35 Nm (60 lbft) @ 2,500 r.p.m.

Ignition   Coil. 12 volt

Fuel System –

Type   Electric liftpump

Type of fuel   Gasoline (petrol)

Air cleaner   Dry. Paper element

Fuel capacity   36.4 litres (8 gall)

Engine Lubrication –

System   Wet sump.Full force feed

Engine Cooling –

System   Pressurised.Thermo-syphon

Wheels & Tyres –

Wheels & rims   4"J x 12" standard commercial disc & rim

Transmission gearbox ratios
Complete range not available. 1st – 3.63:1 4th – 1.00:1

Transfer gearbox
2 speed (integral with engine/gearbox unit)

Transfer gearbox ratios
1.00:1 constant mesh. 1.64:1 low gear

Axles front & rear
Spiral bevel

Axles ratio   4.41:1

Overall ratios 4.41:1 high.26.25:1 low

Differential   2. In front & rear axle

Propeller shaft
Open drive shaft.Hotchkiss type to rear only

Brakes –

Type   Hydraulic

Parking or hand brake
Mechanical rear wheels

Trailer brake   Overrun type

Suspension –

Front & rear   Independent-torsion bar

Shock absorbers Double acting hydraulic telescopic, front & rear

Electrical Equipment –

Generator or alternator
Generator 12 volt DC 22 amp

Batteries   12 volt 45 amp hour (lead acid)

Suppression   F.V.R.D.E. spec. 2051 Appendix D1. Schedule B

Body -
Length, width, sides (height)
                    Not available
Steering -
Type   Rack & pinion

Turning circle 10.5 metres (415 in.)
Towing -
Attachment   Not fitted
Variants   None

TRAILER SPECIFICATIONS

A large variety of trailers of $\frac{1}{4}$, $\frac{1}{2}$ and $\frac{3}{4}$ ton capacity are in the Services whilst others are under development or assessment. These trailers cover a number of duties in association with the Land Rover. Such duties include -
Cargo, water purification, plant, sensitivity test equipment, water tanker, welding set & equipment, folding types of trailers and power drive trailers.
Specifications of a large variety of these types of trailer are contained in the following pages.

TRAILER No. 1   Two wheeled
        1 ton cargo.
        Power driven

This is a two wheeled trailer, capable of being towed with or without mechanical drive to the vehicle. The chassis frame is steel welded construction with semi-elliptic spring suspension mounted on a differential (live) axle. The tow eye and power drive coupling are interchangeable to suit the role. When the tow eye and hook are fitted, the brake operation is vacuum/mechanical. The power driven trailer role, when coupled to a Land Rover four wheel drive vehicle, gives a six wheel driven train with considerable higher mobility over soft terrain, particularly if gradients are to be climbed. Still in service.

SPECIFICATION
Height (top of chassis)
                0.68 metres (27 inches)
Height (top of body)
                1.24 metres (49 inches)
Width   1.8 metres (71 inches)
Length   3.02 metres (119 in.)
Unladen weight (est.)
                613 kgs (1,350 lb)
Laden weight   1,630 kgs (3,590 lb)
TECHNICAL DATA
Wheels & Tyres -
Wheels & rims   6.50L x 16 standard
                commercial type wheels
                & rims

Tyres, size	9.00 x 16 lightweight cross country tread pattern. 6 ply rating	

Tyres, size	9.00 x 16 lightweight cross country tread pattern. 6 ply rating
Suspension	Semi-elliptic longitudinal leaf springs with Aeon rubber spring aid
Shock absorbers	Double acting hydraulic telescopic

Transmission -

Propeller shaft	Open drive
Axle	Spiral bevel
Axle ratio	To be the same as the towing vehicle's rear axle ratio

Brakes -

Service	Mechanical overrun. Vacuum/mechanical when power drive is effected
Parking or hand	Mechanical

Jacking -

System	3 support jacks, 1 at front, 2 at rear

SPECIFICATION

Dimensions -

Height	1.051 metres (41.5 in.)
Width	1.409 metres (55.5 in.)
Length	2.965 metres(116.75 in)
Track	1.213 metres (47.75 in)

Weights -

Unladen weight	342.3 kgs (754 lb)
Laden weight	896 kgs (1,974 lb)

TECHNICAL DATA

Wheels & Tyres -

Wheels & rims	4.50E x 16 W.D. divided pattern disc & rim
Tyres, size	6.50 x 16 cross country tread pattern. 6 ply

Suspension -

Type	Semi-elliptic longitudinal leaf springs
Brakes -	Overrun hand brake
Jacking -	3 folding jacks, 1 at front, 2 at rear

TRAILER No. 2   Two wheeled
½ ton sensitivity test No. 2
        (SAGW)

TRAILER No. 3   Two wheeled
¾ ton 1000 gall per hour
water purification plant

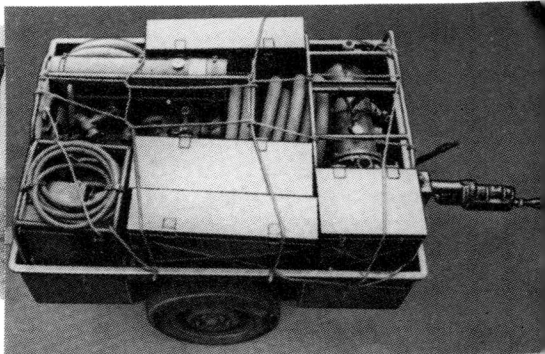

This is a standard trailer of ½ ton capacity cargo. The standard body was modified to accommodate special test equipment - a SAGW system.
Introduced in 1962, replaced by supply trailer SAGW of 1 ton capacity, designed to carry packaged missiles for the ET316 system. No longer in service.

This trailer is of pressed steel welded frame construction with normal semi-elliptic suspension mounted on a single tubular axle. Braking on both wheels is by an overrun mechanism from the draw eye. The draw bar is reversible to suit varying heights of the prime mover. An all steel body of watertight construction is installed with a water purification plant capable of giving an average output of 1,000 gallons of filtered and sterilised water per hour against a total static head of 80 feet. Developed in 1966. In service at the present.

SPECIFICATION

Dimensions -

Height	1.245 metres (49 in.)
Width	1.38 metres (55 inches)
Length	2.92 metres (115 in.)
(including draw bar)	
Track	1.21 metres (47.5 in.)

Weights -

Unladen weight	Not available
Laden weight	917 kgs (2,018 lb)

TECHNICAL DATA

Wheels & Tyres -

Wheels & rims	4.50E x 16 W.D. divided pattern discs & rims
Tyres, size	6.00 x 16 cross country tread pattern. 6 ply

Suspension -

Type	Semi-elliptic longitudinal leaf springs

Brakes -

Service	Mechanical overrun
Parking or hand	Mechanical
Jacking -	3 folding legs attached to chassis, 1 front 2 rear.

TRAILER No. 4   Two wheeled
    ½ ton cargo Mk. 1

This trailer is of steel welded frame construction with semi-elliptic spring suspension mounted on a tubular axle. Braking on both wheels is actuated by an overrun mechanism from the draw bar eye. The draw bar is reversable to suit any varying height of the prime movers. An all steel cargo body of watertight construction is fitted. The body is provided with wheel valances, a duck-board floor and canopy to protect the load. Standard electrical equipment is provided.

Introduced in 1962. No longer in service. Replaced by ¾ ton cargo trailer. (No. 9)

SPECIFICATION

Dimensions -

Height	0.99 metres (39 inches)
Width	1.37 metres (54 inches)
Length	1.82 metres (72 inches)
Track	1.21 metres (47.75 in.)

Weights -

Unladen weight	199 kgs (438 lb)
Laden weight	797 kgs (1,558 lb)

TECHNICAL DATA

As for Trailer No. 3, except

Jacking -	Support legs attached to chassis

Variants -

Special equipment:
With the body removed and separate mud flaps and wings fitted, the trailer can be used for the carriage of specialist equipment, e.g. water tank, generating plant, etc.

TRAILER No. 5   Two wheeled
    ½ ton machinery pack

The chassis is a standard Service 10
cwt, 2 wheeled pattern. The machine and
hand tools are housed in an aluminium
container. The side panniers of the
container are removeable for easy
man-handling. Legs are provided so that
the container can be free standing and
operate away from the trailer. The
container can be carried in a Land Rover
cargo vehicle. This solution to provide
repair facilities for forward R.E.M.E.
detachments was under assessment in 1962
and the container pack was in prototype
form. Not proceeded with.

SPECIFICATION
Dimensions -
Height   1.49 metres (58.75 in.)
Width   1.37 metres (54 inches)
Length   2.9 metres (114 inches)
Track   1.22 metres (48 inches)
Weights -
Unladen weight Not available
Laden weight   814 kgs (1,792 lb)
TECHNICAL DATA
As for Trailer No. 3, except
Jacking   3 folding legs
Container body -
Dimensions -
Length   1.371 metres (54 in.)
Width   1.09 metres (43 inches)

Sides (height) 0.9 metres (35.25 in.)
Weights -
Laden weight   495 kgs (1,092 lb)

TRAILER No. 6   Two wheeled
    Lightweight fibreglass

The base of this trailer is of sandwich
type construction with inner and outer
skins of glass fibre reinforced poly-
ester resin, with the cavity filled with
rigid polyurethane foam plastic. Mild
steel reinforcing plates are bonded in
position during the body construction
and are used for attachment of the
suspension, towbar, jacks and both
lifting and lashing eyes. Suspension is
by means of rubber torsional units with
trailing arms.

Under development and assessment in
1962. Not proceeded with and not in
service.

SPECIFICATION
Dimensions -
Height   1.03 metres (40.5 in.)
Width   1.37 metres (54 inches)
Length   3.10 metres (122 in.)
(including towbar)
Track   1.17 metres (46 inches)
Weights -
Unladen weight 330 kgs (728 lb)
Laden weight   1,245 kgs (2,744 lb)

TECHNICAL DATA
Wheels & Tyres -
Wheels & rims 5.50F x 16 W.D. divided
              pattern disc & rim
Tyres, size   7.50 x 16 cross country
              tread pattern. 6 ply
Suspension -
Type   Independent rubber
              torsional units with
              trailing arms
Brakes -
Service   Mechanical overrun
Parking or hand Mechanical handbrake
Jacking -
System   3 folding stabilising
              jacks are fitted, 1
              front & 2 rear
Special Equipment - Lifting & lashing
              points are fitted for
              transportation by air
Variants   None

TRAILER No. 7   Two wheeled
  ¼ ton lightweight folding

The chassis and body of this trailer are
of integral construction, the body being
centrally hinged to enable it to be
folded into a box form. Mounting points
for the suspension and drawbar are
incoporated in the chassis. The suspension utilises rubber torsional units
with trailing arms. Brakes are not
fitted.
Development and assessment in 1962. Not
continued and not in service.

SPECIFICATION
Dimensions -
Height   0.64 metres (25 inches)
Width   1.35 metres (53 inches)
Length   1.27 metres (50 inches)
Track   1.17 metres (46 inches)
Length (including towbar)
             1.96 metres (77 inches)
Weights -
Unladen weight 91 kgs (200 lb)
Laden weight   363.2 kgs (800 lb)
TECHNICAL DATA
Wheels & Tyres -
Wheels & rims 3.50 x 12 standard
              commercial discs & rims
Tyres, size   5.20 x 12 cross country
              tread pattern. 6 ply
Suspension -
Type   Rubber torsional units
              with trailing arms
NOTES: The trailing arms and wheels are
retractable for ease of packing during
transit. The drawbar and mudguards are
detachable and are stowed inside the
folding body during transit.

TRAILER No. 8   Two wheeled
  ¼ ton foldaway

This trailer, of Danish design built in
Britain under licence, is made to be
readily collapsed and stowed in the
prime mover when not in use. After
removing the wheels and drawbar, the

body can be folded into a pack about 1.09 x 0.41 x 0.25 metres (43 x 16 x 10 inches), the total operation taking less than 3 minutes. The light alloy body had a slatted floor to ease folding and the shallow sides are hinged. The axle is permanently attached to the body and is fabricated from steel tube, as is the drawbar.

Developed and assessed in 1962. Not continued with and not in service.

SPECIFICATION

Dimensions -

Height	1.02 metres (40 inches)
Width	1.3 metres (51 inches)
Length	1.33 metres (52.5 in.)
Length (including towbar)	
	2.18 metres (86 inches)
Track	1.18 metres (46.5 in.)

Weights -

Unladen weight	97.6 kgs (215 lb)
Laden weight	351.8 kgs (775 lb)

TECHNICAL DATA

Wheels & tyres -

Wheels & rims	2.125 x 8 well base rim Standard commercial discs
Tyres, size	4.00 x 8 standard commercial tread patt.

Suspension -

Type	Independent. Laminated spring steel torsion bars with trailing arms

Special Equipment -

Plywood sideboards can be clipped in position if the load is bulky.

TRAILER No. 9   Two wheeled
     ¾ ton cargo

This two wheeled trailer is of ¾ ton capacity and is of welded steel construction. The body is watertight and is capable of floating and shallow water fording. The trailer is fitted with stabilising jacks, one at the front and two at the rear. Lashing points are provided for securing the load and for a canvas tilt cover. The size and weight of the trailer allows for airportability in transport aircraft in Service use. Still in service

SPECIFICATION

Dimensions -

Height	0.94 metres (37 inches)
Width	1.425 metres (56 in.)
Length	2.92 metres (115 in.)
Track	1.2 metres (47 inches)

Weights -

Unladen weight	356 kgs (784 lb)
Laden weight	1,118 kgs (2,464 lb)

TECHNICAL DATA

Wheels & Tyres -

Wheels & rims	4.50 x 16 standard commercial disc & rims
Tyres, size	6.50 x 16 standard tread pattern 6 ply

Suspension -

Type	Semi-elliptic longitudinal leaf springs & Aeon rubber spring aid
Shock absorbers	Double acting hydraulic telescopic

Brakes -

Service	Mechanical overrun
Parking or hand	Mechanical connection to overrun

Jacking -

	3 telescopic jacks; 1 front, 2 rear

TRAILER No. 10   Two wheeled
   ¼ ton tanker water
    (100 gallons)

This trailer is basically an FV 2360 type chassis, fitted with a 100 gallon water tank, which is of welded steel construction, incorporating a large manhole with a hinged cover for access purposes. It is fitted internally with anti-surge baffles and has provision for fitting an immersion heater. Back flushing, draining and filling cocks are provided. A semirotary hand pump is provided to fill the tank with filtered water at maximum rate of 10 gallons per minute.
Introduced in 1966. Still in service.
SPECIFICATION
Dimensions -

Height	0.94 metres (37 inches)
Width	Not available
Length	2.92 metres (115 in.)
Track	1.2 metres (47 inches)

Weights -
Unladen weight 564 kgs (1,240 lb)
Laden weight   1,017 kgs (2,240 lb)
TECHNICAL DATA
Wheels & tyres -

Wheels & rims	4.50E x 16 standard commercial discs & rims
Tyres, size	6.50 x 16 standard tread pattern. 6 ply

Suspension - .

Type	Semi-elliptic long-tudinal leaf springs & Aeon rubber spring aids
Shock absorbers	Double acting hydraulic telescopic

Brakes and Jacking -
As Trailer No. 9
Towing -   Draught eye

TRAILER No. 11   Two wheeled
   ¼ ton welding set lightweight
    trailer mounted

This is a basic ¼ ton two wheeled cargo trailer fitted with a lightweight welding set. The trailer is of welded steel construction and is fitted with stabilising jacks.
The welding set is powered by a Deutz 2 cylinder type F2L310 compression ignition engine rated at 18 b.h.p. @ 3,000 r.p.m. The open circuit is 15 - 35 volts D.C. and a current of 200 amps is available on a 75% duty cycle. Ferrous and non-ferrous metals can be welded using an M.I.G. shielded arc gun employing a gas shield of either Argon or carbon dioxide.
SPECIFICATION
Dimensions -

Height	1.67 metres (66 inches)
Width	1.43 metres (56 inches)
Length	2.92 metres (115 in.)
Track	1.2 metres (47 inches)

Weights -
Unladen weight Not available
Laden weight   1,068 kgs (2,352 lb)
TECHNICAL DATA
Wheels & Tyres -

Wheels & rims	4.50E x 16 standard commercial type rims & 5 stud discs
Tyres, size	6.50 x 16 standard tread pattern. 6 ply

Suspension -

Type	Semi-elliptic long-tudinal leaf springs & Aeon rubber spring aids
Shock absorbers	Double acting hydraulic telescopic

Brakes, Jacking and Towing
As Trailer No. 10

Trailer 10   Trailer 11

Military Vehicles &
Engineering Establishment

The M.V.E.E. was formed on 1st April, 1970, by the amalgamation of two establishments already carrying out work on wheeled and tracked vehicles – the Fighting Vehicles Research and Development Establishment (F.V.D.R.E.) [at Chertsey, with ranges at Kirkcudbright, Scotland] and the Military Engineering Experimental Establishment (M.E.X.E.) [at Christchurch]. The M.V.E.E. has its headquarters at Chertsey, with the old M.E.X.E. station still active in Dorset and ranges at Kircudbright.

The Estalishment is responsible for research, design and development of all types of prime movers, wheeled and tracked vehicles, also trailers with and without power drive. This covers vehicles for all the Armed Services and for certain Government Depertments and engineering equipment for the Royal Engineers. The work includes feasibility studies for new equipment, the preparation of concept designs and the sponsoring and control of design detail and prototype manufacture undertaken by industrial companies under development contracts.

The Establishment is split into two responsibilities each under a Deputy Director under the control and guidance of the Establishment Director. The Senior Deputy Director is responsible for development projects and research programmes covered by 4 divisions, Future Systems, Sub-Systems, Vehicle Engineering and Engineer Equipment. The other Deputy Director is a military officer and, in addition to being a

Aerial view of part of the
Main Test Track Area

Part of the Alpine Course,
Bagshot Heath

Senior Military Officer, he is responsible for trials and evaluation of all vehicles and equipment and for the Establishment workshops. Additionally, the Establishment has a planning branch, responsible for the preparation and costing of future programmes and progress reporting. The administrative branch, under the Secretary is responsible for finance, including estimates and contracts, stores procurement and personnel. Services available to all divisions are the design and drawing offices, a graphic section, libraries, and report sections, a production contracts section, drawing stores and a print room. There are also film and photographic sections equipped for the production of photographs and complete sound films of trials in laboratory, on the test tracks, and in all trials environments from arctic to tropical.

It is interesting to speculate what endurance tests the Land-Rover, like other wheeled vehicles, underwent at the Military Vehicles Engineering Establishment at Chertsey before it was accepted for Service use.

The main test track at Chertsey consists of a 2 miles perimeter circuit of high grade asphalt road, 35 feet wide, roughly eliptical in plan, laid on a cement stabilised subgrade strong enough to permit continuous running by the heaviest tracked or wheeled vehicles. There is a straight and level section $\frac{1}{4}$ miles long, but the remainder of the course generally follows the undulations of the site. There is an inner loop across the south-east curve of the perimeter circuit built to the same specifications. This loop was laid out to make the most effective use of a small hill feature, in order to give a series of sharp curves and short, but steep, gradients.

Situated within the main perimeter are a number of specially designed test facilities used to calibrate vehicle performance. A number of these can also be used for accelerated reliability trials on certain design aspects of a vehicle. These facilities permit close control of a test, under accurately repeatable conditions.

The more important of these facilities are the Suspension Test Courses, the Test Slopes, the Wading Pit and the Tilting Platform. There are also

a number of gauges for determining belly clearance, suspension artic-
ulation limits, landing craft and aircraft loading clearances and similar
parameters of vehicle design. The Winch Test House, together with its
supplementary equipment, provides a means of assessing a number of
other aspects of vehicle design apart from its primary purpose of winch
and winch gear testing.
The four test slopes are used for climbing and braking trials. Two of
these have a concrete surface and gradients of 1 in 4 (25% or 14
degrees) and 1 in 3 (33.3% or 18 degrees), the others have special
surfaces to give adhesion for tracked vehicles and gradients of 1 in 2
(50% or 26 degrees) and 1 in 1.73 (57.8% or 30 degrees). there is a slip
pad of flat circular asphalt of an area of 500 feet in diameter on
which tests can be conducted on steering, drawbar pull and turning
circles.
running parallel with the suspension circuits is a camera track from
which high-speed photography of suspension movements can be taken.
There are two other test courses: the Bagshot Test Course and Long
Valley at Aldershot
These two sites provide natural courses which simulate certain severe
Service conditions. they are primarily used to assess reliability and
robustness, but they are also valuable for comparitive assessment of
vehicles under these conditions and for obtaining crew reaction.
Bagshot Heath Test Course –
There are three courses here, laid out over a severely eroded area of
sandy gravel. The Rough Road Course is a two mile pot holed circuit of
water bound macadam construction, which is used by all wheeled
vehicles. The Alpine course provides a three and a half mile circuit of
natural surface track containing many steep gradients. It is used by
both light wheeled vehicles and light tracked vehicles. The Red Road
Course is a flat cross country track about two and a quarter miles
long. Its surface is also natural and is used by all classes of wheeled
vehicles as well as by light tracked vehicles. The surfaces of these
courses are not repaired, just left to deteriorate, giving conditions
encountered during conflicts and underdeveloped overseas countries.
Long Valley, Aldershot
Two courses, one about four miles long and the other about two and a
half miles long, over generally flat area of sand and sandy gravel, are
used respectively for wheeled and tracked vehicles. These courses are
quite natural and have no maintenance work done on them. Their
surface condition is very dependent on the weather and the effects of
any previous traffic. In wet weather they provide very rough muddy
cross country going, in dry weather they are extremely dusty. The soil
in this area is particularly abrasive and rapidly reveals any lack of
protection of exposed suspension, steering or drive components. Each
Land Rover submitted for testing endures most of these tests and
reliability courses. Satisfaction must be obtained on suspension, handling
and steering endurance, also wading tests to ensure a limited accep-

tance without stopping the engine or the driveability of the vehicle through water. Reliability tests on the long main and Bagshot courses must be cleared for acceptance by the Services. Again, the slopes give the degree of climbing ability the Land Rover is capable of, not only being able to climb the slopes, but prove its 'metal' on stop and re-start.

Launch of a Swingfire missile from the crew-portable palletised infantry version of the Swingfire system on a Land Rover. Swingfire's unique automatic 'gathering' of the missile into the controller's field of view allows the launcher to be concealed from the enemy in natural cover. The controller is also some distance from the launcher. Together these features give Swingfire a degree of battle-worthiness unrivalled by competing systems

Armoured personnel carrier. Land Rover 2.77 metre wheelbase with special armoured body by Short Brothers, Belfast.